# NOLO'S

---

# PARTNERSHIP

---

# MAKER™

---

BY ATTORNEY TONY MANCUSO AND MICHAEL RADTKE

**NOLO PRESS**      **BERKELEY**

## Your Responsibility When Using a Self-Help Law Materials

We've done our best to give you useful and accurate information. But laws and procedures change frequently and are subject to differing interpretations. If you want legal advice backed by a guarantee, see a lawyer. If you use Nolo materials, it's your responsibility to make sure that the facts and general advice they contain are applicable to your situation.

## Keeping Up To Date

To keep its books and software up to date, Nolo Press revises them periodically. If you send in your registration card, we'll notify you when we publish a new version of this software, and you'll be able to buy it at a substantial discount. Registered owners also receive a free two-year subscription to our quarterly newspaper, the *Nolo News*, which contains update information about all our books and software. To find out if a later version of any Nolo book or program is available, call Nolo Press at (510) 549-1976 or check the catalog in the *Nolo News*.

We also offer a 25% discount off the purchase price of any new Nolo book if you turn in any earlier printing or edition. (See the "Recycle Offer" in the back of the manual.)

FIRST EDITION

| | |
|---|---|
| First Printing | SEPTEMBER 1992 |
| Book Design | JACKIE MANCUSO |
| Package Design | TONI IHARA |
| Editor | RALPH WARNER |
| Index | MARY KIDD |
| Proofreading | ELY NEWMAN |
| Printing | DELTA LITHOGRAPH |

ISBN 0-87337-165-8

## *Nolo's Partnership Maker* License

This is a software license agreement between Nolo Press and you the purchaser, for the use of *Nolo's Partnership Maker* program and accompanying manual. By using this program and manual, you indicate that you accept all terms of this agreement. If you do not agree to all the terms and conditions of this agreement, do not use *Nolo's Partnership Maker* program or manual, but return both to Nolo Press for a full refund.

### Grant of License

In consideration of payment of the license fee, which is part of the price you paid for *Nolo's Partnership Maker*, Nolo Press, as licensor, grants to you the right to use this manual and enclosed program to produce partnership agreements for yourself, your business partners and your immediate family, subject to the terms and restrictions set forth in this license agreement.

### Copy, Use and Transfer Restrictions

*Nolo's Partnership Maker* manual and program are protected by copyright. You may not give, sell or otherwise distribute copies of the program to third parties, except as provided in the U.S. Copyright Act and by the terms of this license. You may not use the program to prepare partnership agreements for commercial or nonprofit purposes, or use the program to prepare partnership agreements for people outside your business partners and your immediate family.

### Commercial Use of This Product

Nolo Press offers a license to lawyers, independent paralegals, small business consultants and other non-lawyers for commercial use of this program. For information, please call Nolo Press at 1-510-549-1976.

## Disclaimer of Warranty and Limited Warranty

This program and accompanying manual are sold "AS IS," without any implied or express warranty as to their performance or to the results that may be obtained by using the program.

As to the original purchaser only, Nolo Press warrants that the magnetic disk on which the program is recorded shall be free from defects and material in normal use and service for 90 days from the date of purchase. If a defect in this disk occurs during this period, the disk may be returned to Nolo Press. As long as you have previously returned the enclosed registration card to Nolo, we will replace the disk free of charge. In the event of a defect, your exclusive remedy is expressly limited to replacement of the disk as described above.

## Term

The license is in effect until terminated. You may terminate it at any time by destroying the program together with all copies and modifications in any form.

## Entire Agreement

By using *Nolo's Partnership Maker* program, you agree that this license is the complete and exclusive statement of the agreement between you and Nolo Press regarding *Nolo's Partnership Maker.*

## Contents

# INTRODUCTION

CHAPTER 1

# *PARTNERSHIP MAKER* USER GUIDE

CHAPTER 2

# INTRODUCTION TO PARTNERSHIPS

**CHAPTER 3**

# PARTNERSHIP AGREEMENT CLAUSES

# APPENDIX

# INTRODUCTION

## A. The Need for a Partnership Agreement

Forming a new business with others is exciting, especially if you have chosen the people wisely with whom you'll share your business energy. But one thing is for sure: no matter how personally close and trustworthy your business associates, you will want to put your new business on a solid legal footing. When forming a partnership, this means preparing a partnership agreement.

The reasons for doing this should be obvious. Future problems can arise and changes can occur in your business. More capital may be needed for expansion or to pay debts; one partner may quit or wish to sell her interest in the business; a partner may become disabled or die, leaving a spouse and children; you may consider adding new partners. Preparing a partnership agreement allows you to set out your methods for handling these possibilities, at the same time that it gives you a chance to test whether you and your partners are comfortable working together to solve questions concerning money and power. If you find that you aren't, its better to change your business plans (or your partners) now to avoid future pain and expense.

# B.  Using the Program

*Nolo's Partnership Maker* allows you to prepare a partnership agreement on your computer with a minimum amount of time and trouble. Within a few minutes, you can run the program, read the introductory help screens and follow the simple program procedures necessary to select and add clauses to your own partnership agreement. The program provides 84 clauses that you can include in your partnership agreement. These clauses contain standard and alternative legal provisions and options that are suitable for the typical partnership business. The program provides step-by-step legal help for understanding each clause and filling in any blanks in each clause.

After selecting and filling in the clauses to include in an initial agreement, use the program menu to print this agreement and pass it out to your potential partners. After allowing plenty of time for their feedback, run the program again and make all agreed upon changes to your initial agreement. You may wish to repeat this process a few times before settling on a final version of your partnership agreement. Once you are satisfied, print the final version of you partnership agreement and have it signed by all the partners.

**SUGGESTED READING**

*Legal Guide For Starting and Running a Small Business* by Steingold. This comprehensive book contains essential information on forming and operating a small business, including sole proprietorships, partnerships and corporations.

*The Partnership Book* by Clifford & Warner. This is the predecessor title to *Nolo's Partnership Maker* software and includes additional background information on partnership law and taxation as well as sample clauses for preparing a limited partnership agreement.

*How To Form Your Own Corporation* by Mancuso. These are step-by-step guides, with forms, for organizing profit, and nonprofit corporations. Included in this series are state-specific books and computer software editions for forming profit corporations in California, Florida, New York and Texas as well as a national nonprofit corporation edition good in all 50 states.

# C.  Using the Manual

Chapter 1 contains the user guide for the program, explaining in detail how to use the program to create a partnership agreement. Much of this information is also contained in the program help system contained in the program, and is accessible by pressing the <F1> from any program screen. We suggest all users skim through this chapter prior to using the program.

Chapter 2 provides a broad overview of partnership law and how it controls the types of clauses included in partnership agreements. This chapter also provides a brief summary of other ways people can combine forces to do business. Read Chapter 2 if you are undecided on forming a partnership or wish basic background information on partnerships.

Chapter 3 contains a numbered listing of all legal clauses contained in the program together with a helpful discussion of each clause. Again, this information is also presented on the screen when you run the program. Some users may wish to refer this printed material to obtain an overview of the clauses included in the program.

The Appendix contains helpful material:

- a consolidated listing of all of the legal clauses contained in the program without the help material. Referring to this listing is a good way to see the legal language of the clauses in one place at one time.

- a sample agreement, titled SAMPLE.DOC. This is a printed listing of a sample partnership agreement included on the distribution disk. This agreement contains all the basic clauses we suggest beginning partnerships use (all fields within clauses have been left blank). To save time and effort, you may wish to load this agreement into the program and use it as the basis for your initial partnership agreement (see the sidebar instructions).

- a listing of the laws (Uniform Partnership Act statutes) enacted in each state. This list will be helpful if you wish to do a little legal research on your own.

**TO LOAD AND USE THE SAMPLE PARTNERSHIP AGREEMENT**

- Install the program as explained in the Quick Start card (or see the User Guide in Chapter 1).
- At the DOS prompt, run the partnership program by typing "partner<Enter>".
- After reading the Introductory help screens, press the <F10> menu key to display the program menu.
- Select the Load command from the Document menu by pressing the <D> followed by the <L> key.
- The name "Sample" should be highlighted in the directory lookup list that appears at the top of the screen (the install program copies this file to the Partnership Maker directory). Press <Enter> to load the SAMPLE.DOC agreement into the program.
- The name of the clauses contained in the sample agreement will be listed in the document panel at the bottom of the screen. Select each clause name in this panel with the arrow keys, then press <Enter> to view the legal and help text for each clause.
- Add, remove and move clauses in the sample agreement, then fill in the blanks in the clauses as explained in the User Guide (Chapter 2) and in program help (press <F1>).
- Rename, save and print your agreement by selecting the appropriate commands from the Document menu.

# D. Please Fill In and Mail the User Registration Card

We have designed *Partnership Maker* to help you create your own partnership agreement with a minimum of time and expense. Still, we recognize that creating such an important agreement is a challenging task and you may have questions not covered by this software package. To help us provide software that meets your needs (and to get a free two-year subscription to the *Nolo News*), please fill in and mail the User Registration card included in the package.

## Icons Used in This Manual

 **Fast Track**

 **Suggested Reading**

 **Warning**

 **Tip**

# PARTNERSHIP MAKER USER GUIDE

# A. Introduction

In this chapter we show you how to install and use *Nolo's Partnership Maker* software. Much of the information presented here, together with additional program information, can be viewed on the screen by requesting program help at any time while running the program (see the sidebar text).

### ACCESSING AND USING PROGRAM HELP

<F1> Program Help is context-sensitive: The <F1> key help system is designed to provide specific help for your current menu item or panel selection. For example, to find out more about the Load command, highlight this command in the Document menu by pressing <F10>, then press <F1>. To learn more about the document panel at the bottom of the screen, select the document panel at the bottom of the screen by pressing <F3>, then press <F1>. If no specific help is available for the current selection, you will be brought to the first screen of help overview.

The other way to access different portions of the help system is to choose the program help command from the Help menu (press the <F10> then the <H><P> keys) then select one of the six help systems (contents, glossary, error messages, keystrokes, overview or panel tutorial).

**The Best Way To Use This Guide**   We suggest you skim through this chapter prior to using the program. Then, use the program help system if you have any questions. If you still have questions or can't find the topic or feature you are looking for in the program help system, come back to this guide and look up the command or feature in the table of contents at the beginning of this guide.

**USER GUIDE CONVENTIONS**

We use the following conventions throughout this chapter to describe program operations:

- The names of keys on the keyboard are shown surrounded by angle brackets—for example, the enter key is shown as <Enter>.

- Combination keys are also shown between angle brackets with a hyphen between them: <Alt-X>. A combination keystroke means to press and hold the first key while pressing the second (hold the <Alt> key while pressing the <X> key).

- Information that the program or DOS displays on the screen is printed in plain Courier typeface in capital letters—for example: `--PRESS ENTER WHEN READY TO CONTINUE--`

- Information that you type on your computer keyboard is shown in Courier typeface capital letters, preceded by the DOS prompt—for example: `C:\>DISKCOPY A: B:.`

# B. Technical Information

## 1. System Requirements

To run *Nolo's Partnership Maker*, you will need the following system configuration:

- an IBM Personal Computer (PC, XT, AT, PS/2) or 100% compatible computer running MS/ or PC/DOS version 3.0 or later

- a floppy disk drive for program installation and backup

- at least 600K of available disk space on a hard disk or floppy disk. If 360K floppy diskettes are to be used, two disks and two drives are required.

- a monochrome or color monitor

- at least 512K of Random Access Memory (RAM) available to the program

- a serial or parallel printer.

## 2. Program Disks

This program is distributed on a standard (720K) 3$^{1}$/$_{2}$" or (360K) 5$^{1}$/$_{4}$" MS-DOS formatted data disk. *Partnership Maker* is a compiled program and does not require another application program (such as BASIC) to be run on your computer.

## 3. Program Files

### a. Distribution Files

The files included on the partnership distribution disk are:

**PARTNER.PAK**   a compressed file containing all *Partnership Maker* files.

**INSTALL.EXE**   a utility program on the distribution disk that decompresses and copies the files in the PARTNER.PAK file to your working disk and directory.

**README**   a text file containing any late additions and/or corrections to the program manual. This file may be viewed with the DOS TYPE command. To view the file, type:

```
B:\>TYPE README <Enter>
```

To print the file, type:

```
B:\>TYPE README >PRN <Enter>
```

## b.  Working Files

The following files are copied to your working disk and directory by the Install program. They are necessary for program operation and should be kept in the same directory:

**PARTNER.EXE**  the *Partnership Maker* program itself.

**NOLO0414.CLS**  a data file containing the legal and help text for the clauses that can be included in your partnership agreement.

**PARTNER.HLP**  contains the primary text for the program overview, glossary and tutorial panel contained in program help system.

**HELPLONG.HLP**  contains the text for the table of contents portion of program help.

**HELPERR.HLP**  contains the list of error messages and their descriptions contained in program help.

The following two files are also copied to your working disk and directory by the Install program but are not necessary for program operation:

**PARTNER.ICO**  the icon used for windows.

**SAMPLE.DOC**  a sample partnership agreement.

In addition, *Partnership Maker* will create the following files as necessary upon first running the program:

**NOLO0414.IX**  an index file that references the NOLO0414.CLS data file. *Partnership Maker* uses it to find and display the legal and help text for clauses you select while using the program.

**PARTNER.IX**  these are index files for the help system files.
**HELPLONG.IX**
**HELPERR.IX**

**PARTNER.INI**  contains the default and user-saved settings for printing, screen colors, sounds and other program settings and options.

### c.  User Files

The following files are produced by *Partnership Maker* when the you create, save and print a partnership agreement:

**DOC File**    *Partnership Maker* saves your partnership agreements in specially formatted files, ending with a "DOC" filename extension. When an agreement is first created, it is named UNTITLED.DOC (you can rename the agreement when it is saved). You can reload and update these partnership agreement files at any time.

**NOTE**    All partnership agreements must end with a DOC filename extension. If the agreement is not given a filename extension when it is saved or loaded, the program supplies the DOC filename extension. If you use another filename extension, it is changed to DOC.

**PRN Text Files**    These are text files that the user can "print" to a file on the disk and load into a word processing program for final formatting prior to sending the file to a printer. *Partnership Maker* gives these files the same filename as the document upon which they are based, together with a filename extension of PRN. For example, if an agreement named PARTNERS.DOC is printed to a text file on the disk, the program will use PARTNERS.PRN as the name of the file.

# C.  Installing and Running *Partnership Maker*

## 1. Make a Backup Disk

Make a backup copy of the program disk and set the original aside for safekeeping. Place the distribution disk in your A: floppy disk drive and place a blank backup disk in the B: drive. At the DOS prompt, type the following:

```
C:\>DISKCOPY A: B:<Enter>
```

to copy the program disk in A: to the backup disk in B:.

**NOTE**   If the disks placed in your A: and B: drives are different sizes, this Diskcopy command won't work. In these cases, use the one-drive Diskcopy procedure shown below.

**Using One Drive**   If your A: drive cannot read the distribution disk, or if you have a single floppy disk drive computer system, you can make a copy using one disk drive. Place the distribution disk in the floppy disk drive (let's assume it is the A: drive) and type the following at the DOS prompt:

```
C:\>DISKCOPY A: A:<Enter>
```

After reading the disk in B: into memory, DOS will prompt you to insert a blank destination disk in the B: drive, then copy the contents of the disk in memory to your destination disk.

## 2. Installing *Partnership Maker* on Your Hard Disk

The files on the *Partnership Maker* distribution disk are stored in a special compressed format to allow them to fit on the distribution floppy disk. You must use the Install program to decompress and copy the *Partnership Maker* program files from the distribution disk to your working disk and directory.

To install *Partnership Maker,* do the following:

- Insert your backup copy of the distribution disk in your floppy disk drive (again, we assume the B: drive).

- Log on to this floppy disk drive and run the Install program by typing

  ```
  B:
  ```

- When the B: prompt appears, type

  ```
  INSTALL<Enter>
  ```

- The Install program will guide you through the installation process. After installation, the partnership working files will be stored in a directory on your hard disk. Unless you specify a different directory, the *Partnership Maker* files will be stored in the PARTNER directory on your hard disk.

**Floppy Disk Users**   You can install and run *Partnership Maker* on one floppy disk drive if it recognizes 5$^1$/4" high density (1.2 Meg) or 3$^1$/2" ( 720K or 1.4Meg) floppy disks. Make sure your destination floppy disk is blank and is formatted in one of these three formats. If you use 360k floppy disks, the program will be installed on and must be run from two floppy disks (you will need *two* floppy disk drives).

# 3. Running the Program

To run the program from the hard disk, first change to the directory where the program files were placed by the install utility:

`C:\>CD PARTNER`

Then at the DOS prompt for the partner directory, type

`C:\PARTNER>PARTNER`

to run *Partnership Maker.*

**DOS NOTE**   If your DOS prompt does not include the name of your working directory ("C:\Partner>") as shown in the above example, type the following command line:

`C:\>PROMPT=$P$G`

This changes the DOS prompt until you turn your computer off. To make this change permanent, include this command line in the AUTOEXEC.BAT file on your hard disk as explained in your DOS manual.

**If Screen Highlighting Is Not Working**   The Install program helps you set up *Partnership Maker* for your graphics adapter card and video monitor so that screen highlighting appears properly. In a small number of cases due to hardware differences, screen highlighting may not be noticeable and you may not be able to tell which item or selection on the screen is the current item. To fix this problem, press <F10><Q><E> to exit the program, then run *Partnership Maker* again by typing the following command line at the DOS prompt:

```
C:\PARTNER>PARTNER /B
```

The /B parameter forces the program to treat your adapter card and monitor as a black and white monitor and should correct the problem.

**NOTE** To switch back to color program operation after typing the above command, you must rerun the program by typing the following command at the DOS prompt:

```
C:\PARTNER>PARTNER /C
```

**Startup Settings and Options** The first time you run the program, it uses the default settings stored in the program for print settings, sounds, colors and other settings and options. When exiting from the program, it creates the PARTNER.INI file to store these options. Once you change and save these settings (by using the Save Options menu command as explained below), the program will use the new settings when you run the program again. If this startup file is deleted a new one will be created with the program's default settings.

**Using 360k floppies** If you use 360k floppy disks and have installed *Partnership Maker* on two floppy disks, insert the disk containing the PARTNER.EXE file in the A: drive and type

```
A:\>PARTNER
```

to run the program.

The program will ask you to specify the path where the NOLO0414.CLS file is located. Place the second *Partnership Maker* disk (created with the install program) in the B: drive, then answer the question by typing

```
B:NOLO0414.CLS
```

in the response panel (you must type the filename exactly).

Finally, make sure to save your program options by pressing the <F10> menu key, followed by the <O> then <S> keys. This saves the location of the

NOLOL414.CLS file in *Partnership Maker* option settings file. The next time
you run the program, you will not need to specify where this file is located.

## a.  Introductory Help Screens

The first time you run *Partnership Maker*, a series of introductory help
screens appear on the display, beginning with the Welcome screen. If you do
not wish to view these screens, select the Start item from the Main menu,
Press <F10> then <S>, and select <M>ain screen. This will force the program
to skip the introductory screens and display the Main Screen that asks you to
choose a category of clauses for your agreement. To change the program to
always skip the introduction screens each time you start the program, select
the Save Options command from the menu, press the <F10><O> then <S>
keys.

```
Press <F1> for help; <F10> for menu. Press <F10><S><M> keys to go to main
screen. Press <F3> to switch active panel; <F4> to shrink/expand active panel.
═══════════════════════════════════INTRODUCTION═══════════════════════════════



                              WELCOME TO

                      NOLO'S PARTNERSHIP MAKER (TM)

                             Version 1.0

                      by Mick Radtke & Tony Mancuso

                 Copyright 1992 by HxD Software & Nolo Press






                      --PRESS ENTER TO CONTINUE--
```

*Partnership Maker* **Welcome Screen**

# D. Basic Program Operations and Features

In this section we provide an overview of legal provisions contained in the partnership agreements and describe the basic program operations necessary to prepare your partnership agreement.

**FOR MORE INFORMATION**
- The program presents specific legal help for each clause and field within a clause as you prepare your agreement.
- For detailed on-line program help (glossary, table of contents, keystroke commands and panel tutorial), select Program Help from the Help menu or press the <F1> function key at any time when running the program.
- For a numerical listing and additional legal help for each partnership agreement clause, see Chapter 3.
- For a printout of a blank agreement with all clauses, see the Appendix at the back of this manual [or print an agreement with the print blank option as found discussed in Menu commands (Section E) below].

## 1. Who Can Use This Program?

*Partnership Maker* can be used by anyone who plans to pool energy, efforts, money or property with others to run a business, produce a profit or share property, or to engage in any type of mutual undertaking or endeavor. It allows you to produce a printed agreement that answers essential questions such as:

- Who will contribute what to the joint enterprise or endeavor?

- If a partner fails to contribute money or perform services, what happens?

- How will profits and losses be divided? Can partners take draws from profits or be paid salaries?

- If a partner wishes to sell out or leave the partnership, who can buy the partner's interest and for how much?

- If a dispute arises, how will it be resolved without costly legal proceedings and lawyers fees?

These and other issues are dealt with and resolved as you use the program to prepare your agreement. Doing this gets your business off to a better start, helps avoid misunderstandings later and makes ending the business easier if you later decide to call it quits.

## 2. What Type of Agreement Can You Prepare?

The partnership agreement starts out with no clauses; you can make it as simple or as complex as you wish by selecting the individual clauses that you wish to include in it. You select a clause to be included in your agreement, then you complete any fields (blanks) in the clause following the instructions on the screen. You repeat this process until you have selected and filled in all the clauses you wish to include in your agreement. You then save and print your agreement for all partners to review and sign.

The program includes clauses that cover essential areas of partnership formation and operation, specifying how the business begins, how ongoing decisions will be handled and how a departing partner will be bought out. Here are several examples:

- Names of the partners and the effective date of the partnership agreement

- Names of the partnership and the partnership business

- The types and amount of capital contributions made by the partners

- How profits and losses and voting powers are divided among the partners

- Partnership work provisions (hours worked, salaries, vacation, etc.)

- Who may sign partnership checks

- The time and place for holding formal partnership meetings

- The manner of purchasing a departing partner's interest and the price that must be paid by the partnership for that interest

- If a dispute among the partners arises, how will it be handled.

Other areas of partnership operation may be handled in a number of ways. To accommodate these differences, the program allows you to choose among one or more alternative clauses. Here are just a few examples of the alternative clauses contained in the program:

- Term of the partnership can be indefinite or last until a specific event or date.

- The formula used to value partnership interests can be based on the partnership's net worth, a set dollar amount, a capitalization of earnings formula, the proceeds actually paid under an insurance policy or an appraisal of the partnership.

- The partnership, a majority of the partners or a specific partner owns the business name if a partner departs or the partnership dissolves.

- If initial contributions are not made, partnership dissolves or partnership continues with or without additional contributions by remaining partners.

## 3. How To Prepare Your Agreement

The process necessary to produce a partnership agreement is simple and consists of selecting a series of partnership clauses and filling in any fields (blanks) that appear in them. At every choice, help text is displayed on the screen to aid you in choosing clauses and filling in blanks.

Here's a step-by-step look at this process:

- The main program screen lists broad categories of partnership clauses, such as Preliminary Clauses, Buy-Out Clauses, etc. You select a category with the arrow keys, then press <Enter>.

```
Select a category with the arrow keys, then press <Enter>.
Press <F1> for help; <F10> for menu; <F3> to switch panel; <F4> to size panel.
═══════════════════════════════MAIN SCREEN══════════════════════════════▲▼═

        PRELIMINARY CLAUSES (1-7)

        CONTRIBUTION CLAUSES (8-16)

        LOANS TO THE PARTNERSHIP (17-18)

        PROFITS, LOSSES AND DRAWS (19-25)

        MEETING AND VOTING CLAUSES (26-30)

        PARTNERS' WORK PROVISIONS (31)

        FINANCIAL CLAUSES (32-41)

        OUTSIDE BUSINESS ACTIVITIES BY PARTNERS (42-44)

        BUY-OUT CLAUSES (45-59)

        INSURANCE & ESTATE PLANNING CLAUSES (60-62)
```

*Partnership Maker* Main Screen

### OPERATION OF THE <ENTER> AND <ESC> KEYS

Throughout most of program, the <Enter> key is used to select a highlighted item or to advance to the next program screen. The <Esc> key is used to terminate the current program operation or to back up one screen.

Example: Pressing <Enter> will select the currently highlighted category, clause or field. Unless you are at the main program screen, pressing <Esc> will close the current category, clause or field panel and bring you back to view the previous panel.

- Each category starts with a brief introduction discussing the types of clauses contained in that category. Below this introduction is a list of the clauses with specific suggestions on using each clause in your agreement. These instructions tell you whether a clause is suggested or optional. Where relevant, you also will be told if a particular clause should be used as an alternative to other clauses in the category.

```
Select a clause with arrow keys, then press <Enter>. Press <F1> for help;
Press <F10> for menu; <F3> to switch panel; <F4> to size panel.
══════════════════════════════════PRELIMINARY CLAUSES══════════════════════════════════▲▼══

    Name clauses: [clauses 1 through 3 suggested]

        1. Names of the partners and effective date.

        2. Name of the partnership.

        3. Name of the business.

    Term of the Partnership: [either clause 4 or 5 suggested]

        4. Until dissolution of partnership [or]

        5. Until specific date or event

    Purposes and Goals of the Partnership: [clause 6 suggested; clause 7
    optional]

        6. Purposes of the partnership

        7. Goals of the partnership
```

***Partnership Maker* Clause Category Screen**

- To see the language of a clause, use the arrow keys to highlight its name, then press <Enter>. The text of the clause will be displayed at the top of the screen; the help text for that clause at the bottom. Press <Enter> again to add the clause to your agreement or press <Esc> to return to the previous Category screen without adding the clause.

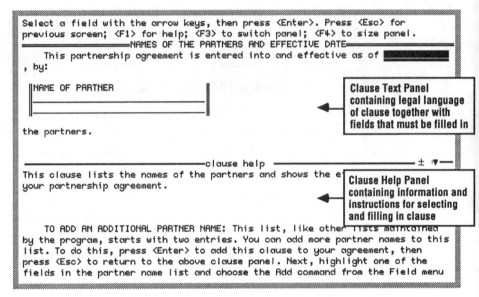

Select a field with the arrow keys, then press <Enter>. Press <Esc> for
previous screen; <F1> for help; <F3> to switch panel; <F4> to size panel.
═══════════════NAMES OF THE PARTNERS AND EFFECTIVE DATE═══════════════
    This partnership agreement is entered into and effective as of ▓▓▓▓▓▓▓
, by:

‖NAME OF PARTNER

the partners.

**Clause Text Panel containing legal language of clause together with fields that must be filled in**

─────────────────────────clause help ───────────────── ± ·▼─
This clause lists the names of the partners and shows the e
your partnership agreement.

**Clause Help Panel containing information and instructions for selecting and filling in clause**

    TO ADD AN ADDITIONAL PARTNER NAME: This list, like other lists maintained
by the program, starts with two entries. You can add more partner names to this
list. To do this, press <Enter> to add this clause to your agreement, then
press <Esc> to return to the above clause panel. Next, highlight one of the
fields in the partner name list and choose the Add command from the Field menu

*Partnership Maker* Clause Text and Help Panels

**NOTE**    When you press <Enter> while displaying a clause, you will be asked
if you wish to add the clause to your agreement *unless you have selected the
Add Clause option from the Automatic menu* (see the Option menu
description in Section E5 below).

• Most clauses contain one or more fields that you must fill in. To fill in a
  field, use the arrow keys to highlight the field, then press <Enter>

**REMEMBER**    The first time you press the <Enter> key, you will be asked if
you wish to add the clause to your agreement.

After you select a field, a field response panel will appear at the top of the
screen with instructions explaining the type of information you should
supply to fill in the field (for example, the name of a partner, a date, time or
place, dollar amount, etc.). Also, the clause help text at the bottom of the
screen will be replaced with more specific field help containing additional
information for filling in the field. Type in your response, then press <Enter>
when you are finished. Your response for this field will be inserted in the
clause.

```
┌─────────────────────────────────────────────────────┐  ┌──────────────────┐
│ Insert the effective date of your partnership agreement.│  │ Field Response   │
│                                                         │  │ Panel for filling in │
│ ▓▓▓▓▓▓▓▓▓▓▓▓▓▓▓▓▓▓▓▓▓▓▓▓▓▓▓▓▓▓▓▓▓▓▓ ◄───────────────│  │ the selected field │
│ ───────────── names of the partners and effective date ─│  │ within the clause │
│     This partnership agreement is entered into and effective as of _____  └──────────────────┘
│ , by:
│ ║NAME OF PARTNER
│ ║├──────────────────────────────────────────────────┤║
│ ║├──────────────────────────────────────────────────┤║
│
│ the partners.
│
│
│ ───────────────────────── field help ─────────────────── ± ───
│ You will normally insert the words "the date of signing of this agreement" in
│ this blank. If the agreement will be signed by different partners on different
│ dates, you should insert the words "the date the last partner signs this
│ agreement."
│
│ However, if you wish your partnership to begin on a particular future date (for
│ example, January 1, 1992), you are free to do so. If you take this approach,
│ make sure that the date specified is on or after the date the last partner
│ signs this agreement.
└─────────────────────────────────────────────────────┘
```

*Partnership Maker* Field Response Panel

Field Response text is automatically adjusted (wrapped) to the size of the panel for screen display or the specified margins for a printed agreement. You can force a new line and insert a carriage return into the text by pressing <Ctrl-Enter>. See the Editing Keys Table below for a complete listing of the editing keys available when typing and manipulating text in a response panel.

**To Expand and Shrink the Field Response Panel**     If you wish to expand the field response panel to display additional lines while making longer responses, press the <F4> key. To shrink the panel back to normal size, press <F4> again. Note that this effects the display of the response panel only. The length of the response is not limited by the size of the panel.

**CUTTING, COPYING AND PASTING TEXT WITHIN A FIELD RESPONSE PANEL**
You can use the Block Control commands listed in the Editing Keys Table to remove, copy and paste blocks of text within a field response panel as follows:
- First mark the start of the block of text by pressing <Alt-M>.
- Move the cursor with the arrow keys to highlight the full text block you wish to work with.
- Then use the <Alt-X> key to remove, or the <Alt-C> key to copy, the text block. This cuts or copies the text to an invisible scrap area maintained by the program.
- The text block in the scrap can now be copied to another location within the current response panel or to another field in another clause. Text copied or cut to the scrap can also be pasted in edited clauses as explained in Section E4.

Using the Edit Menu Instead of Keystrokes: The program's Edit menu is enabled when filling in a field. In other words, you can mark, remove, copy and paste text blocks in a response panel by pressing the <F10> key to display the menu and then selecting the appropriate command from the Edit menu. For further information on marking and manipulating blocks of text, see Section E4.

- Continue selecting any other fields in the clause with the arrow and <Enter> keys and fill them in the same way.
  **NOTE** When you first view a clause, the first field in the clause is automatically highlighted for you; after you fill in a field, the program highlights the next field in the clause.

- After filling in all fields in a clause, press <Esc> to return to the Category screen to select, review and add other clauses to your agreement.

- As you add clauses to your partnership agreement, they are added to the document panel at the bottom of the screen. This panel is named UNTITLED.DOC to start, and contains the names and the order of the clauses that you add to your agreement. In effect, this document panel is your partnership agreement.

## EDITING KEYS TABLE

When typing or changing information in a field response panel (or an edit panel as discussed in Section E4 below), you can use the following editing keys:

### Cursor Movement

| | |
|---|---|
| <Arrow Keys> | move the cursor up, down, right and/or left |
| <Home> | move the cursor to the beginning of the line |
| <End> | move the cursor to the end of the line |
| <PgUp> | scroll the text up within the panel |
| <PgDn> | scroll the text down within the panel |
| <Ctrl-Home> | go to the first line within the panel |
| <Ctrl-End> | go the last line within the panel |
| <Ctrl-PgUp> | go to the top (beginning of first line) of the text |
| <Ctrl-PgDn> | go to the bottom (end of last line) of the text |
| <Ctrl-[left arrow]> | move the cursor one word left |
| <Ctrl-[right arrow]> | move the cursor one word right |

### Editor Control

| | |
|---|---|
| <Enter> | end editing, save changes made |
| <Esc> | end editing, abandon changes |
| <Ctrl-Enter> | insert a carriage return |
| <Insert> | toggle between insert and overtype mode |
| <F4> | expand or shrink the panel |

### Text Deletion

| | |
|---|---|
| <Back Space> | delete one character to the left |
| <Delete> | delete one character at current position |
| <Ctrl-Y> | delete current line |
| <Ctrl-Back Space> | erase all text |

### Block Control (Removing, Copying and Pasting Text)[†]

| | |
|---|---|
| <Alt-M> | mark the block start |
| <Alt-U> | unmark block |
| <Alt-X> | remove marked block and place in the scrap |
| <Alt-C> | copy marked block into the scrap |
| <Alt-V> | paste block from scrap into text starting at the current cursor position. |

[†]You also can use the Edit menu commands to mark, unmark, remove, copy and paste text blocks in field response and edit panels (press the<F10> and <E> keys, then select the appropriate command).

**NOTE** When you first run the program, the Main screen is at full size and hides the untitled blank document panel. However, as soon as you add a clause to your agreement, load a previously created agreement or use the <F3> or <F4> keys to switch panels or change their size (as explained in Section 4a below), the document panel appears at the bottom of the screen.

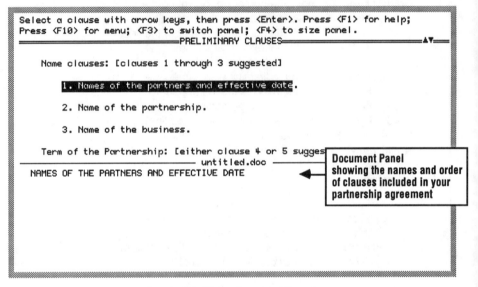

*Partnership Maker* Document Panel

## DOCUMENT PANEL CLAUSE SYMBOLS

There are four symbols that can precede the clause names listed in your document panel, as follows:

— a dash means that none of the fields in the clause have been filled in

▨ a shaded box means that some, but not all, of the fields in the clause have been filled in

■ a filled-in box means that all of the fields in the clause have been filled in

¶ this symbol means that you have edited the legal language of the clause (see Section E4 below).

- You can move, remove or edit the clauses in your agreement by making the document panel the active panel by pressing the <F3> key, highlighting the name of a clause in the document panel, then selecting the Move, Remove or Edit Clause command from the Clause menu.

- To save or print your agreement, first make the document panel the active panel by pressing the <F3> function key. Then show the menu bar by pressing the <F10> function key and use the arrow keys to choose the Save or Print command from the Document menu. Among the options offered under the Print command is the ability to save your agreement as a text file on the disk. You can load this file into your word processor for special formatting and printing if you wish.

- After saving your agreement and quitting the program, restart the program and reload your agreement by selecting the Load command from the Document menu.

- For further information on each menu command, see Section E below.

# 4. Other Program Operations and Features

## a. Working With Multiple Panels

As you've seen, the program frequently splits the screen into an upper panel and a lower panel. In this section we explain how to select and perform program operations within one of the panels shown on the screen.

For further information, select and read the panel tutorial contained in program help (press <F1> or select Program Help from the Help menu, <F10><H><P><P>).

## 1. Selecting between two panels

When two panels appear on the screen at the same time, one of the panels is active and the other is inactive. You can only scroll text, make selections or enter information in the active panel. When you display a clause, the program puts the clause in the upper panel and legal help text in the lower panel. If you wish to make the bottom panel the active panel, press the <F3> function key. When you want to switch back to the top panel, press <F3> again.

 To easily tell which panel is active, check its title bar. If it has two horizontal lines and the name of the panel is in capital letters, it is the active panel. Inactive panels have only one horizontal line and use lower case letters in their title bar.

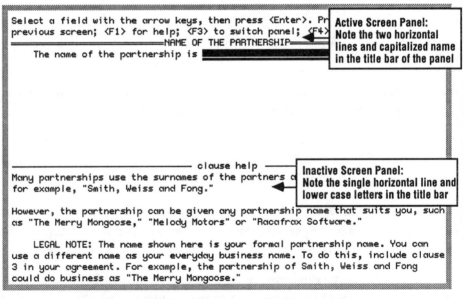

*Partnership Maker* **Screen With Active and Inactive Panels**

## 2.  Expanding and shrinking the active panel

You can expand the active panel to cover the entire screen at any time by pressing the <F4> function key. Pressing <F4> a second time shrinks the panel back to its original size.

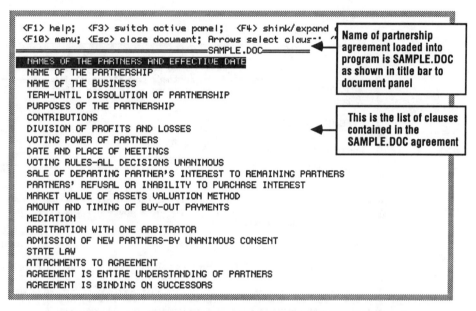

Expanded Document Panel Showing Clauses in SAMPLE.DOC Agreement

## 3.  Scrolling or paging text within the active panel

If there is additional text that does not fit in a panel, you will see a downward pointing triangle at the right of the panel's title bar. Press the down arrow to scroll downward and view the hidden text. Press the up arrow to go back to the top line of text.

**Remember**   You can only scroll text in the active panel. If the arrow keys do not scroll the text in a panel, press <F3> to switch panels.

You can use the ± page commands to step quickly through all of the help text for the fields within a clause (instead of selecting each field to read the help text for each field separately). Specifically, if the title bar of the clause help panel at the bottom of the screen contains a ± symbol, then press <+> to step forward through all of the field help panels for each of the fields within the clause (or press <-> to cycle backwards through these panels).

```
Press <F10> for menu; <F3> to switch panels; Press <F4> to size panel.
Use arrow keys to scroll; Press <±> to page through field help.
───────────── names of the partners and effective date ───────────
   I. This partnership agreement is entered into and effective      A downward pointing
__, by:                                                             triangle means that
                                                                    more text within the
 NAME OF PARTNER                                                    active panel can be
                                                                    viewed by pressing
                                                                    the down arrow key

the partners.


══════════════════════════CLAUSE HELP══════════════════════  ± ═▼═
This clause lists the names of the partners and shows the effective date ▲f
your partnership agreement.
                                                                    The ± symbol means that
                                                                    additional panels
    TO ADD AN ADDITIONAL PARTNER NAME: This list, like other        containing field help text
by the program, starts with two entries. You can add more pa        for the current clause can
list. To do this, press <Enter> to add this clause to your a        be viewed by pressing the
press <Esc> to return to the above clause panel. Next, highl        + or - key
fields in the partner name list and choose the Add command f
```

**Clause Help Panel With Scrollable Text**

## b. Using the Program Menu

Many of the program's operations, such as loading, saving or printing an agreement, are performed by selecting a command from the program menu.

•  To display the menu bar at the top of the screen, press the <F10> function key. A line of text will appear just below the menu bar explaining the function of the highlighted menu item on the menu bar.

- Use the arrow keys to highlight an item or command then press <Enter> (or type the first letter of the menu item or command). The item or command will be carried out or you will presented with a submenu with additional commands or terms. Select the subcommand or item in the same way by pressing the first letter of the subcommand or item using the arrow keys followed by <Enter>.

- To return to the program from the menu without performing a command, press <Esc> one or more times until the menu bar disappears or simply press the <F10> key once.

- When the menu bar is active and displayed on the screen, it takes control of all keystrokes entered. Other parts of the screen are not accessible when the menu bar is showing.

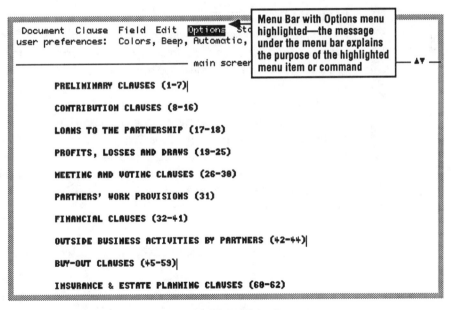

*Partnership Maker* Menu Bar

**Disabled Menu Items and Commands**    Some items or commands in the menu bar may be dimmed (or in the inactive color specified in the custom color options). These are disabled menu items: choices that are not accessible at the moment because of the current state of the program. For instance, you cannot save a document (and the Save command will be dimmed) if there are no clauses in your document panel at the bottom of the screen. Similarly, the Clause, Field and Edit items on the menu bar are dimmed (and cannot be selected) if the document panel is not the active panel.

**To Activate a Dimmed Menu Item**    The usual cause for items appearing dimmed in the menu bar is that your document panel is not the active panel. Press the <F3> function key to switch to your document panel, then press <F10> again to show the menu.

**MENU MEMORY FEATURE**

The program remembers and highlights your last sequence of menu items, commands and subcommands. In other words, you only need to press <Enter> one or more times after displaying the menu bar to repeat your last menu operation or to access the same menu item, command or subcommand.

For example, if you set the foreground color for normal text under the Custom item of the Color command in the Options menu (by pressing <F10><O><C><C><N><F> (Options-Colors-Custom-Normal-Foreground), you can repeat this operation and make another color selection from the same menu by pressing <F10>, then pressing <Enter> five times and choosing a new color. For other keystroke shortcuts, see the explanation of macros in Section G below.

For an explanation of each of the menu commands, see Section E below.

## c.  Automatic Data Entry

When data is entered into a field that occurs in more than one clause in the program (such as the name of the partnership), it is automatically transferred to corresponding fields in the other clauses. Changing the information in any one of these linked fields changes the information in the other fields.

For example, when the name of the partnership business is entered in the Business Name clause (clause 3), this name will be carried over to and inserted in any other clauses that use this name [for example, the Control of Business Name clauses (clauses 63 through 66)].

**Local Entry of Data**     In rare cases, you may wish to override this automatic data entry feature, for instance to fill in a field that you do not wish to have carried over to other fields in your agreement. To do this, select the clause, then highlight the field that you wish to fill in within the clause. Instead of pressing <Enter> to select the field, press <Shift-Enter> (hold down <Shift> while pressing <Enter>) or select the Local command from the Field menu, <F10><F><L>. The program will ask if you wish to make your response local. If you select "Yes," your response for this field will not be linked to any other field in any other clause.

You can change a response back to global by highlighting a field and selecting the Global command from the Field menu (press <F10><F><G>). The program asks if you wish to delete your local response; select Yes to make it global. The program deletes the local response and replaces it with the global response (if any) specified in other clauses in your agreement.

## d.  Entering Data in Lists

Some fields within clauses have vertical bars surrounding them and have room for multiple responses (for example, the partners' names). These fields are lists and have the capability to be expanded if more names are necessary.

Entry of data into a list field is the same as for a normal field. However, in addition, the Field menu can be used to add or remove fields to the list.

**EXAMPLE**    Clause 1 (Names of the Partners) contains a list for the entry of the names of the partners. As with all beginning lists, space is initially allocated for two entries. If you wish to add the name of a third partner, highlight any field in the list with the arrow key, then select Add from the Field menu (press <F10><F><A>). A new field will be added to the bottom of the list, ready for you to insert the name of the third partner. Since automatic data entry applies to lists, this operation need only be done once. All other lists for your partners' names in other clauses will contain this third line, showing the name of your third partner.

## e.  Creating and Using Macros

The program allows you to define and playback a macro—a sequence of key-strokes. To define a macro, do the following:

- Press <Alt-F10>. A message will appear on the third line:
  `"Define Macro. Enter keystroke to define."`

- Press the key that you wish to assign to your macro. You should use function keys or key combinations with the <Alt> or <Ctrl> key that are not otherwise used by the program. We recommend that you use the <F5> through <F9> function keys. The message will change to:
  `"Macro now recording! Alt-F10 to end."`

 Certain keys that are used by the program are protected from being redefined with macros: <Esc>, <Enter>, <F10>, <Alt-F10>. All other keys used by the program are NOT protected from being redefined. Care should be taken that keys such as <Home>, <End>, the function or arrow keys, and the editing keys should not be redefined. Also, it makes no sense to create a macro using a letter for your definition key, since it prevents you from using that key for data entry. For instance, if you define a macro for the letter 'a', you would no longer be able to enter the word "apple" into a field since the 'a' would invoke your defined macro.

- Now  press the keystrokes that you wish to use in your macro. Typically, you will type the <F10> key followed by the letters necessary to invoke a menu command.

- End the macro definition by pressing <Alt-F10> again. This time the program reports:

`"Macro recorded."`

Your macro can then be played back whenever you wish by pressing the function key or key combination assigned to your macro.

**SAMPLE MACRO DEFINITION**

If you occasionally use the Print menu to set special left and right margins (at columns 15 and 55 respectively), you can define a macro to do this for you by pressing the following key sequence:

| | |
|---|---|
| <Alt-F10> | begin macro definition |
| <F8> | define function key <F8> as the key assigned to this macro |
| <F10> | display menu bar |
| <D> | select Document menu |
| <P> | select Print submenu |
| <M> | select margins setting |
| <L> | select left margin setting |
| <Ctrl-Back Space> | move cursor left to start of line |
| <15> | set left margin at column 15 |
| <Enter> | finish setting left margin |
| <R> | select right margin setting |
| <Ctrl-Back Space> | move cursor left to start of line |
| <55> | set right margin at column 55 |
| <Enter> | finish setting right margin |
| <F10> | hide menu bar |
| <Alt-F10> | end macro definition |

Now that the macro is defined, whenever <F8> is pressed, the above macro will be replayed, setting the left and right margins.

Macros can be saved from one session to another by selecting the Save Options command from the menu bar.

**To Undefine a Macro**    Use the same steps for defining a macro. Press <Alt-F10> to start the macro recorder. Press the letter for the previously defined macro, then press <Alt-F10> to end the macro redefinition. The letter will be restored to its original empty state.

**Use Menu Memory Instead of a Macro**    The program remembers and reselects your last series of menu selections when you access the menu (by pressing <F10>) and press <Enter>. Use this feature of the program, instead of a macro, to repeat your *last* series of menu bar selections.

# E.  Menu Commands

In this Section, we explain the purpose and effect of each of the menu commands.

**Remember**    To display the program menu bar, press the menu key <F10>. Then highlight a menu item or command by using the left or right arrow keys and press <Enter> to execute the command or display a submenu. Alternately, type the first letter of the item or command you which to invoke. After performing a command, the menu bar will disappear and you will be returned to the program. To return to the program without implementing the highlighted menu item or command, press the <Esc> key one or more times or press the <F10> key once.

**EXAMPLE**    To access the menu bar, and select the Load command under the Document menu, press the <F10><D><L> key sequence.

For further information on using the menu bar, see Section D4b above.

# 1. Document menu

## a. Load

The program prompts you for the filename of the document that you wish to load, and displays the name of the current directory at the top of the screen followed by "*.DOC" at the cursor. This is the current criteria that the Load command uses to list files in the directory lookup list. This list appears just under the filename criteria message. Use the left or right arrow keys to scroll the files in the directory list and highlight the name of the file you wish to load, then press <Enter>.

To type in the name of a file yourself or to change the criteria that the Load command uses for the directory lookup list, press <Esc>. Then, type the name of the file or the new criteria that the Load command should use to list files. Remember: You do not need to specify a filename extension of DOC; the program assumes all document files end with this extension. If you type a different extension, the program will substitute ".DOC" in its place prior to attempting to load the file.

**EXAMPLE**     Press <Esc> and type "PARTNER" to load the file named PARTNER.DOC in the current directory. Or type "MYNAME*" to have the directory lookup list show all .DOC files with filenames beginning with these characters.

## b. Save

This command saves your partnership agreement (which contains the clauses listed in the document panel at the bottom of the screen) in a document file on disk. You are prompted to input a filename for the saved document. The initial name given to your agreement is UNTITLED.DOC. If no path is supplied, the file will be saved on the current disk and directory. .DOC is automatically used as the filename extension. If you specify a different

extension, .DOC will be substituted as the filename extension of the saved
partnership agreement.

## c. Rename

This command prompts you for a new filename for your partnership agreement. The new name appears in the title bar of the document panel and will
be used as the name of the document when it is saved. Note that the new
name is not written to disk until you perform a Save command from the program menu. Renaming the document does not erase or rename the original
document file; instead, a new file will be written to disk with the new name.

## d. Print

When you select the Print menu from the menu bar, a submenu appears with
the following items:

### 1. Printer

Choose this item when you wish to print your document on your printer.

Your partnership agreement will be printed according to the settings
discussed below (margins, controls, title, blanks). You can monitor the status
of your printout by watching the clause names in the document panel on
your screen. As each clause in your document is sent to the printer, the name
of the clause is highlighted on the screen.

**To Cancel or Pause Printing**    Press <Esc> if you wish to stop printing. The
printout will pause and you will be asked if you wish to abandon the printed
output. Select "Yes" to stop printing or "No" to resume printing.

## 2. Disk

Select this item to send the printout to a disk file.

You will be prompted for the name of the file to be created (the default is the filename of your document with a .PRN extension). If the file already exists, you will be warned and prompted for verification to overwrite the file or to reenter a new filename. The document is output to a disk text file according to the current print settings. As with standard printing, when you print to disk, the name of each clause in the document panel is highlighted on the screen as it is sent to the disk file.

The disk files produced by *Partnership Maker* are text-only files (sometimes refereed to as ASCII files) that can be opened, edited and printed using most PC word processing programs. These text files contain alphanumeric characters and standard control characters (carriage returns, line-feeds, form-feeds, etc.) No formatting such as headers, footers, bold, italics, centering or special font information is included.

**Margins and Control Settings for Printing a Text File to Disk**    We suggest you set left margin setting to "0," the control form feed option to "no page breaks," and the control carriage return option to "paragraph" prior to printing your document to disk. By doing this, you eliminate unnecessary hard spaces, carriage returns and form-feed characters in your text file and make it much easier for you to set margins and page breaks using your word processor's formatting commands. See the subsections below for further information on print option settings.

## USING *PARTNERSHIP MAKER* DISK TEXT FILES WITH YOUR WORD PROCESSOR

After saving one or more documents as text files, quit the program and open your disk text files with your word processing program. Below are basic instructions for opening text files with a few of the most popular MS-DOS word processing programs.

### WordPerfect (v. 5.1)

- Type WP at the DOS prompt to run the program. Press any key to open a blank WordPerfect screen. Press <F5>, input the name of the directory containing your partnership document file (usually "C:\Partner"), then press <Enter> to access the list of files in this directory.

- Move the cursor with the arrow keys until the name of your partnership .PRN text file is highlighted. Then press <1> to retrieve the file. WordPerfect will report "DOS Text Conversion in Progress" and open the document after a few seconds.

- Set left and right margins <Shift-F8><2><5>, center<Alt-F4><Shift-F6>, and bold heads <Alt-F4><F6> as appropriate and print the file <Shift F7> when you have finished reformatting the file. Save your changes by pressing <F7>.

### Microsoft Word (v. 5.5)

- Run Word at the DOS prompt and select the Open command from the File menu.

- Select the partnership directory and type the name of your text file in the file name box. Press <Enter> to open the file.

- Use the ribbon to change styles, fonts, font sizes and character formatting (select Ribbon from the View menu to turn the ribbon on) or apply formatting with commands from the Format menu.

- Print and save the document by choosing these commands from the Document menu.

**WordStar (v. 3.2)**

- Type WS to run WordStar and display the Opening menu. Type <d> followed by the name of the text file you wish to edit. Press <Enter> to open the file.

- Set margins by using the <Cntrl-O><L> and <Cntrl-O><R> commands. Toggle justification by using the <Cntrl-O><J> command. Line spacing can be set with the <Cntrl-O><S> command.

- To reformat the file based on your new margins and line spacing, place the cursor at the beginning of the text and type <Cntrl-Q><Q><B>. If you are asked to hyphenate and do not wish to, simply type <Cntrl-Q><Q><B> again or turn off hyphenation with the <Cntrl-O><H> command.

  Centering can be applied to heads with the <Cntrl-O><C> command; to bold a head, type <Cntrl-P><B> before and after the head.

- To print the file from the edit mode, type <Cntrl-K><P>, then type the name of the file and press <Enter>. To save your work and return to the Opening menu, press <Cntrl-K><D>.

**NOTE**    If you decide to use your word processor to edit or add language to your agreement, make sure your changes conform to the applicable provisions of the Uniform Partnership Act in effect in your state (see the appendix at the back of the manual for a listing of your state's partnership laws).

## 3.  Margins

Use this command to set the number of spaces or lines the program uses for top, bottom, left and right margins when printing your agreement. The Page command sets the number of lines printed on each page (including top and bottom margins). The Width command specifies the number of characters across the page (this includes the left and right margins).

**DEFAULT PRINT SETTINGS**

The Print commands are initially set with the default values listed below. You can change these settings and perform the Save Options command to use them in future sessions

| | |
|---:|:---|
| **Top Margin** | 6 lines |
| **Bottom Margin** | Line 58 |
| **Left Margin** | 11 spaces |
| **Right Margin** | 65 spaces |
| **Page** | 66 lines |
| **Width** | 80 spaces |

If you print on standard letter-size ($8^{1}/2$" X 11") paper using 12 point type, these defaults should work fine for you.

Note that some printers have automatic pagination features that skip the folds in fan-fold paper. This feature needs to either be disabled on the printer, or your printing options should take this into account (by setting the Form Feeds setting in the print Control menu to "No Page Breaks").

## 4.  Control

The Control command allows you to specify settings used to control printing.

**Port**   Allows the selection of PRN, LPT1, LPT2, LPT3 as the printer port or device. The standard DOS printer device is PRN, which will output printing to the current printer port (usually LPT1). However, users with two printers or those with special setups may wish to select another choice here.

**SERIAL PRINTERS**

Those users who have serial printers need to configure DOS for their printer from the DOS prompt. This is done with the MODE command:

```
C:\>MODE LPT1=COM1
```

For more information on the MODE command, see your DOS manual.

**Carriage Return**   This selection provides you with the choice to place a carriage return at the end of each paragraph (this is the default), or place a carriage return at the end of each line within a paragraph.

This choice only matters if you wish to print your document to a text file (by choosing the Disk command as explained below). If you do, you probably will want to stay with the default here, since most word processors expect carriage returns at the end of paragraphs, not at the end of each line. Use the Line command here to place carriage returns at the end of each line only if you are printing your agreement to a text file that will be read in by a line editor (such as the MS/DOS EDIT or EDLIN programs).

**Form Feed**   Use this setting to specify how the program will advance the printout to the next page. Most printers work best when each page of your printout ends with a form feed character (this is the default setting here). However, if you plan to print your file to disk, you may wish to change this option to specify that each page will end with a series of carriage returns or without any breaks between pages.

**Start Page**   Choose this setting to specify the first page the program will use when it starts printing. You will be prompted to input the page number from which to start. The default starting page is page 1.

**End Page**   Choose this option to limit the printed output up to a certain page. You will be prompted to input the page number that will cause the output to cease. The default here is page 999 (which means your printout will go to the end of your agreement).

## 5.  Title

This item allows you to specify the name that will appear in the heading of your printed partnership agreement. The default title is "PARTNERSHIP AGREEMENT." If you select this command, you will be prompted for a new title for your printed agreement. If you save your settings (by choosing the Save Options command), the program will use this new name as the heading for partnership agreements printed in future sessions.

**NOTE**   The title specified here appears in your printout only. The name of the document file that contains your partnership agreement is specified separately when you use the Save command from the Document menu.

### 6. Blanks

This option allows you to print your document with your filled in responses or with blanks appearing in the fields within the clauses in your agreement. The default setting is to print your agreement with your responses in the fields. If you wish to print a blank agreement to pass out and discuss with your partners, choose Blanks. Then, all fields within clauses will appear with blanks (underlines) in place of any responses supplied to the program.

 Make sure to fill in all fields in all clauses included in your final agreement before it is printed and signed by the partners.

### 7. Save Options

Select this item to save your print settings together with other program settings and options. Program options and settings are saved (in the PARTNER.INI file) when this command is selected, so any colors or other program settings and options will be saved along with your print margins and control settings. For a complete list of savable program options and settings, see Section E5 below.

**NOTE**    The print control options for the starting and ending pages, as well as the option to print blanks in your printed agreement, are not saved with this command. If you wish to specify a range of pages to print, or to print a document with blanks, you must specify these settings each time you run the program.

## 2. Clause menu

The items under this menu allow you to perform special operations on the clauses within the document panel at the bottom of the screen. The clauses that appear in this panel are the clauses that you have selected and added to your partnership agreement. When you print your agreement, the clauses are printed in the order that they appear (from top to bottom) in this panel.

## a. Move

This selection is used for changing the position of a clause within your agreement. It is only operational when the document panel is the active panel on the screen. If you have loaded or created a document but the document panel is not the active panel (does not appear at the bottom of the screen or does not have a highlighted name and double menu bar), press <F3> to make it the active panel before using this command.

After making sure that the document panel is the active panel, do the following to move clauses within your partnership agreement:

*   Use the arrow keys to highlight the clause that you wish to move.

*   Display the menu and activate the Move command by typing <F10><C><M>.

*   Use the up and down arrows to position the highlighted clause to its new location in your partnership agreement.

*   Press <Enter> to fix the new position of the moved clause.

## b. Remove

This command is used to delete a clause from your partnership agreement. As with the Move command, your document panel must be the active panel for this command to function (if necessary, press <F3> to display and make the document panel active).

Once the document panel is the active panel, do the following to remove clauses within your document:

*   Use the arrow keys to highlight the clause that you wish to remove from your partnership agreement.

*   Press <F10><C><R> to display the menu and perform the Remove command. Press <Enter> to remove the clause from the Document panel.

You cannot undo this command so make sure you really want to remove a clause from your agreement before performing this command.

## c.  Edit Clause

This command allows you to edit the legal language of a clause. First make sure the document panel containing the clauses in your agreement is the active panel (if necessary, press the <F3> key, then highlight the name of the clause you wish to edit, then select the Edit Clause command by pressing the <F10><C><E> keys.)

This opens a full-screen edit panel containing the legal language of the clause. You can then delete and insert characters in the clause by using the editing keys listed in the Editing Key Table.

Once you have made your changes to the text of a clause within an edit panel, press <Enter> to have the program close the edit panel and accept your changes to the clause. If you wish to cancel your editing session and go back to the unedited version of the clause, press <Esc> instead.

After editing a clause, a paragraph symbol (¶) appears to the left of the clause name in the document panel.

 **Important**  Once a clause has been edited, the program does not keep track of the fields in the clause or provide legal help for these fields (help text for the entire clause does, however, still appear in the bottom screen panel). In other words, if you decide to edit a clause, only the exact language you specify will appear from then on in the clause when you select it from your document panel. You will not be prompted for nor receive any help in filling in any fields remaining in the edited version of your clause. Further, the program will not link any of your responses in the edited clause to similar fields in other document clauses.

**EXAMPLE**  If a clause that contains the partners' names is edited, these names and the edited text become permanent as the edited clause. If you add a partner name to the partner name list in a different (unedited) clause, the edited clause will not reflect the newly-added partner name.

**To Discard an Edited Clause**    You can discard an edited clause and replace it with the original version of the clause by reselecting the name of the clause from the clause selection panel at the top of the screen. After filling in any fields in the new, non-edited clause, press <Enter>. The program will ask you if you wish to replace the edited version of the clause in your document. Select "Yes" to replace the edited clause with the new clause.

**Using Edit Commands**    While an edit panel is open, you can use the programs special Edit commands in the menu bar to remove, copy and paste blocks of text within the clause or from one clause to another. See Section E4 for a further discussion of these commands.

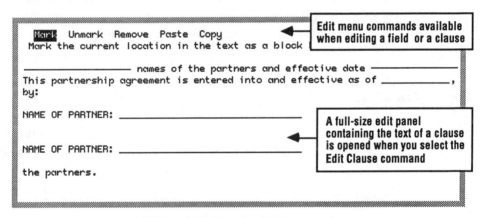

**Edit Panel With Menu Bar Edit Commands**

## d. Numbering

The Numbering command determines the type of notation used to order the clauses when displaying clauses listed in your document panel and when printing your partnership agreement.

Here are the choices:

**Roman**   use roman numerals (I, II, III...)

**Arabic**   use "normal" numbers (1, 2, 3, etc.); this is the default setting

**Caps**   use capital letters (A, B, C, etc.)

**Lower**   use lower case letters (a, b, c, etc.)

Note that the Roman system inherits the upper or lower case of the current number system when you select it. Thus, if you select Lower, then reselect Roman, the numbers generated will be (i, ii, iii, iv, etc.).

**NOTE**   Only clauses that have been included in the document will appear on the screen with a clause number. If you view a clause prior to including it in your partnership agreement, it will not be numbered.

## 3. Field menu

**Add**   This command adds a new field to a list selected within the active clause panel. The new field is added to the end of the list and is made the current highlighted field.

**Delete**   Removes a selected field from a list within the active clause panel.

**NOTE**   Lists always have at least two fields. This means that you cannot delete the last two fields in a list.

For further information on using lists, see Section D4d, Entering Data in Lists, above.

**Global**   *Partnership Maker* normally treats all field responses as "global"—to save user input, whenever you insert information in a field, that information is automatically carried over and inserted in other fields in your agreement that require the same information. For example, when you supply or change the name of your partners or partnership, these responses are treated as global responses and are automatically inserted in any other fields in your agreement that contain the name of your partners or partnership.

As explained below, you can override this feature and choose instead to make a field response "local" so that the information you supply for a field will only be used in the current clause. If you have made a field local, you can change the field back to a global response by highlighting the field with the arrow keys, then selecting this Global item from the Field menu. Once you do this, any information supplied in the field will again be carried over and inserted in corresponding fields in other clauses in your agreement.

**Local**   Highlight a field with the arrow keys, then select this command to make your response local and limit it to the current clause only. As explained above, this means that your response in the field will not be carried over to any corresponding fields in other clauses in your agreement.

**Use the Local Command in Special Cases Only**   Normally you will wish to have your responses treated globally to save typing and have your responses inserted in related fields in other clauses in your agreement. In other words, use the Local command in special situations only where you want to make sure your response in not inserted in fields in other clauses in your agreement.

# 4. Edit menu

The Edit item in the menu allows you to mark, unmark, remove, paste and copy blocks of text when filling in fields within clauses and when editing the legal language of clauses.

All removing, copying and pasting of text blocks using the Edit commands is done through the "scrap." This is an area of memory that the program uses to store text blocks.

**NOTE**   To use these commands to edit the legal language of a clause, you must first use the Edit Clause command from the Clause menu to open an edit panel for a clause as described in Section E2c above. To use these commands to edit a previous response placed within a field within a clause, you must first highlight the field and press <Enter> to open up the response panel for the field.

**Keystroke Equivalents**   All Edit commands can also be performed by using the block control keystrokes listed in the Editing Key Table.

After you have opened an edit clause or a field response panel, do the following:

- Position the cursor under the first letter of the text you wish to operate on, then select the Mark command from the Edit menu (<F10><E><M>) or press <Alt-M> to mark the beginning of the block.

- Use the arrow keys to move to the end of the block. As you move the cursor, the text characters in the block will be highlighted on the screen.

- After highlighting the entire text block, select the Remove or Copy command from the Edit menu (<F10><E><R> or <F10><E><C>) or hold down the <Alt> key and press <X> or <C> to remove or copy the marked text to the scrap. Removing a text block removes the text from the panel and places the text in the scrap. Copying a block simply copies the highlighted text to the scrap without removing the marked text from the panel.

- Move the cursor to another location within the panel. Select the Paste command from the Edit menu or hold down the <Alt> key and press <V> to paste the text block stored in the scrap to the new cursor position.

The Edit commands (or the alternative Block Control keystrokes) are operative from one edit clause panel or field response panel to another. For example, you can copy a block of text from one edited clause, close its edit clause panel, edit another clause, then paste the block from the scrap into the second edit clause panel. Likewise, you can paste the text on the scrap into the response panel for a field in any of the unedited clauses in your agreement (an unedited clause is one listed in the document panel at the bottom of the screen that does not have a "¶" symbol to the left of the clause name).

# 5. Options menu

The various commands and subcommands under the options menu control settings that are used by the program to display colors, produce sounds and control other aspects of program operation. Below, we look at each item that appears in the Options menu.

**Beep**   Choose this item to change the sound that your computer speaker makes whenever a program warning sound is made. There are five possible sounds to choose from (plus no sound at all).

**Colors**   There are a number of choices here to personalize the colors displayed in various parts of the screen during program operation. There are three preset color schemes, plus a black and white only mode. A fourth Custom choice here allows you to set the foreground and background colors and the intensity level for nine separate areas of the screen.

**Automatic**   This item allows you to set the program to perform certain operations for you. Each item may be turned on or off, as follows:

> **Save Doc**   When this setting is on, the program will automatically save your partnership agreement document before exiting to DOS. When this setting is off (this is the default), you are asked whether you wish to save an open document before exiting the program.

> **Add Clause**   When on, this setting automatically adds a new clause to a document when <Enter> is first pressed while viewing a clause. When off (this is the default), the program asks before adding a new clause to a document.

**Delay**   Use this item to specify the number of seconds the program waits before displaying timed status and error messages. The default delay here is one second.

## CUSTOM COLOR CHOICES

**Normal**        used to display standard text (help and clause panel text) on the screen.

**Active**        used to color text that may be selected by the user. Selectable items are those that can be activated by highlighting them with the arrow keys, then pressing <Enter>. Note that the settings here affect the color of items that are not currently selected by the user. To change the color setting for the currently selected item on the screen, choose the Current color setting described below.

**Inactive**      used to color text which is displayed in the menu bar but is disabled and not available for selection by the user.

**Current**       used to highlight the currently selected item on the screen (for example, the current field in a clause panel or the currently selected menu item).

**Field**         used to display underlines (blanks) and user-supplied text that appears in fields within legal clauses.

**Menu**          used to set off menu commands, items and menu help that appear in the top two lines of the program screen.

**Document**      used to color document panels.

**Edit**          specifies colors used to display text appearing in edit panels.

**Help**          for program and legal help panel text.

**Warning**       for program warning messages that appear, when necessary, in the third line of the screen.

**Save Options**   Use this command to save the current Option menu settings; beep, colors, automatic functions, message delay as well as other user settings are saved with this command (see the sidebar text for a full list of program settings and options). Program options and settings are saved in the PARTNER.INI file. This file is reloaded and used by the program each time you run the program. In other words, unless you change your options or settings while running the program, the saved values in this file will be used to set your screen colors, sounds and other options each time you run the program.

**NOTE**   If the PARTNER.INI file is deleted, the program creates a new
PARTNER.INI file containing the default settings when you run the program.

### OPTIONS AND SETTINGS SAVED BY THE PROGRAM

The following options and settings are stored in the PARTNER.INI file. They can
be changed by the user and are saved in the PARTNER.INI file when the Save
Options command is performed:

The first group are set from the Options menu as follows:

- Sounds, colors and time delay for program messages
- Whether documents are automatically saved and clauses automatically
  added to your agreement without separate prompts from the program

The next group are set from the Print command under the Document menu:

- Printing margins and control (printing port, use of carriage returns and form
  feeds)
- Title of printed agreement

The remaining saved options are set from separate menu items or program
operations:

- The first screen displayed each time the program starts (Introductory or
  Main screen)—set from the Start menu.
- The default pathname used by the program for user files—set from the
  Load, Save or Rename command in the Document menu
- Macros defined by the user with the <Alt-F10> keys
- Where the NOLO0414.CLS file is located. This is only important if you install
  and run *Partnership Maker* on two 360k floppy disks. In this case, the
  NOLO0414.CLS file will be placed on a separate program disk.

**NOTE**   The Print command in the Document menu also has a Save Options
command that can be used to save all program options and settings.

**Reset Options**   Use this command to have the program reset itself to the
color, sound and other options and settings saved in your PARTNER.INI file.
This command can come in handy if you've made some option or setting
changes during the course of the current program session and you wish to
reset the options to the options and settings in effect when the program
started.

# 6. Start menu

This command allows you to go directly to the following program screens:

**Introduction**    This choice takes you to the first introduction screen (the Welcome screen). The Welcome screen is immediately followed by a series of introductory screens that explain program operation and use.

**Main Screen**    This selection takes you to the Main Program screen where you select categories of clauses to review and include in your partnership agreement.

# 7. Help menu

The program provides different types of help to assist you in using the program. If you select Program Help from the Help menu, you are given the following choices:

**Contents**    A partial listing of program topics in narrative form.

**Error Messages**    This is a listing and explanation of error messages that can appear during program operation.

**Glossary**    A listing of selectable program topics that can be individually viewed.

**Keystrokes**    An explanation of keys that function during program operation.

**Overview**    This takes you to a Help Overview screen from which you can select any of the specific types of program help (Contents, Error Messages Glossary, Keystrokes or Panel Tutorial).

**Panel Tutorial**    This is a series of on-screen tutorials that explain the basic program operations of opening and closing panels, making selections and scrolling text.

**NOTE**   If the program reports an unrecoverable error, restart the program and select the Errors item from the Program Help menu (press <F10><H><P><E>). You can also press <F1>, then select the "Error" item from the first overview page. Then select the error reported by the program and read the description and possible solution given on the screen. If the suggested solution for the specific error does not help, call Nolo Press technical support (see Section F below).

**NOTE**   The following error can occur before the program is fully loaded, and thus no access to the online help system will be possible:

**Video Adapter**
*Message*      Video adapter board type not recognized.
*Meaning*      The program could not determine the type of adapter used in
                   your computer.
*Solution*     Call Nolo Press Technical Support.

Remember, using the Help menu is just one way to access Program Help; the other way is using the <F1> key. <F1> help is context-sensitive and will bring you to the help screen for your current menu selection or panel. If specific help is not available for the current selection or panel, the <F1> key will bring you to the first screen for Help Overview.

**Legal**   This item allows you to receive legal help for a clause while viewing the clause list that appears in the opened document panel at the bottom of the screen; (normally, you must select a clause and open a clause panel in order to receive legal help for a clause).

If the document panel is the active panel, you can highlight any one of the selectable clause names that appear in the panel, then select Legal Help from the menu to view the legal help for the clause and the fields contained within the clause. Using this option is a quick way to access the legal help for all clauses displayed in an open document panel, without having to select and open each clause separately.

 If your document panel is hidden or inactive, press <F3> to switch to the document panel and make it the active panel.

**To Cancel Help or Backup Through Help Screens**   Use the <Esc> key to cancel help and return to the program or to backup through the help screen sequence that you have just selected. Pressing the <F1> key also cancels help and returns you to the program.

## 8. Quit menu

Use the Quit command to exit the program. You will be asked to confirm that you wish to exit the program.

**Important—Make Sure to Quit the Program**   The program will prompt you to save a document that is opened when you quit the program (or it will automatically save the document if the Automatic Save option is turned on). If you switch off your computer without choosing the Quit command, you will lose work performed during the current session that was not explicitly saved by you.

Except when viewing program help, you can quit the program by pressing <Ctrl-C>. This is the same as choosing Quit from the program menu.

# F.  Technical Support

Nolo Press maintains a customer support line for answering technical questions related to *Partnership Maker.* The telephone number to call and hours of operation are as follows:

1-510-549-1976   Tech Support representative
                 Monday through Friday, 9 to 5 Pacific time

1-510-548-5902   Fax

To help identify and solve your particular problem more efficiently, we ask that you do the following before calling our customer service line:

1. Rerun the program and look up any error reported by the program in the error list contained in Program Help (press <F1> then select Error Messages or press <F10> to display the menu, then press <H><P><E>).

2. If the error list does not provide a solution to your problem, check the manual, and particularly this user guide, to make sure you are using the program correctly.

3. If you still have the problem, write down as much of the following information as you can before calling technical support:

   • make of your computer: if it's an IBM clone, the type of CPU (8086, 286, 386, etc.).

   • the version of DOS you are running.

   • make of your BIOS. This is the name that appears on the screen when you boot your computer. Some machines and configurations will not display this information.

   • type of monitor: color, monochrome, black/white, LCD, etc.

- type of video adapter card: VGA, EGA, CGA, etc.
- amount of RAM and any TSR (memory resident) programs installed.
- what was on the screen *before* the problem happened?
- what keys did you press?
- what happened?

# INTRODUCTION TO PARTNERSHIPS

In this chapter we first discuss the principal ways of organizing a business and provide more detailed information on partnerships. If you are undecided on whether to form a partnership, this overview material may help you with your decision.

 If you are sure that you want to form a partnership and already understand the legal basics of this form of business organization, go on to Chapter 3.

# A.  Your Choices

There are four forms of ownership for profit-making businesses:

- Sole proprietorship

- Corporation

- Limited partnership

- Partnership

If you wish to co-own a business, obviously a sole proprietorship won't work. Nevertheless, let's review all of these options.

# B.  Sole Proprietorships

We will discuss sole proprietorships very briefly since they are not designed to operate businesses with more than one owner. A sole proprietor is a business with one owner. The owner may hire (and fire) employees. She may also even arrange for them to receive a percentage of the business profits as part of their wages, but she remains the sole owner. The owner—and the owner alone—is personally liable for all the debts, taxes and liabilities of the business, including claims made against employees acting in the course and scope of their employment. The business does not pay taxes as an entity; the owner reports and pays taxes on the profits of the business on her own individual income tax returns.

Two good sources of information on how to start and operate a small sole proprietorship are *Legal Guide for Starting and Running a Small Business* by Steingold (Nolo Press) and *Small-Time Operator* by Kamaroff (Bell Springs Press available through Nolo Press).

**Being Your Own Boss**   The main advantage of a sole proprietorship is that since there is only one boss (you), many potential conflicts are eliminated. The disadvantages reflect this same reality—there is only one person (you, again) to assume the burdens of owner and boss. If you get sick, or want time off, or simply want to share the responsibility of decision making with some-one else, you're likely to be stuck unless you are lucky enough to find an employee who is as trustworthy and responsible as you are. Deciding to be the only boss is often a question of temperament. Some people like, and need, to run the whole show, while others want or need the resources and strengths that co-owners can bring.

In deciding whether to operate a business as a sole proprietorship or to adopt a form of shared ownership such as a partnership, a business founder may be inclined to choose shared ownership because she wants to bind key employees to the business by giving them an equity stake. While it may make great sense to allow important employees to become co-owners, either as partners or stockholders, this is not the only way that dedicated and talented employees can be encouraged. A profit-sharing agreement within the frame-work of the sole proprietorship may be a good alternate approach, at least until you see if you and the key employees are compatible over the long term.

When the owner dies, a sole proprietorship legally ends. By contrast, in theory at least, a partnership and a small corporation can continue under the direction of the surviving owners. However, in practice, a sole proprietor who wants his business to continue beyond his death can leave the remaining assets (after paying off its debts, of course) to whomever he chooses. If that person wants to continue to operate the business as a new legal entity, he is free to do so.

# C.  Corporations

We'll discuss corporations in more depth, because they are the major alternative form to partnerships available to owners of a shared business.

A corporation is created by filing articles of incorporation with the appropriate state agency, usually the secretary or department of state. Once this is done, the corporation comes into legal existence.

A corporation is a legal entity which exists separately from any of its owners. In theory, a corporation involves three groups:

- directors who manage the business

- officers who run or oversee day-to-day business operations

- shareholders who own the business.

In many states, one person alone may fill all required corporate positions and own, organize and operate the corporation by herself.

### SOME STATES AUTHORIZE CLOSE CORPORATIONS

Some states allow small corporations, known as "close" corporations, to adopt a shareholders' agreement that allows the owners to operate the corporation informally, to divide profits and losses as they see fit (not necessarily in proportion to stockholdings), and to restrict transfers of stock in the corporation to outsiders (sometimes stock restrictions are imposed on close corporation shareholders as a matter of law). Shareholders' agreements of this sort result in a corporation being operated very similar to a partnership.

Despite their flexibility, close corporations are not popular. To begin with, most incorporators wish to rely on, rather than dispense with, normal corporate rules and procedures (board and shareholder meetings, ownership interests proportionate to shareholdings, etc.) Secondly, the tax status of close corporations is a little fuzzy in some areas (S corporation tax status may not be available to some close corporations). Finally, most incorporators wish their shares to be freely transferrable or restricted pursuant to a custom-tailored buy-sell provisions, not according to blanket prohibitions contained in the close corporation statutes.

The bylaws of a corporation, like a partnership agreement, cover the basic legal and procedural rules for operating the business.

Corporate shareholders have limited liability for the corporation's debts or obligations. Normally, the most each shareholder can be liable for, or lose, is the amount of his investment (the amount used to buy stock in the corporation). We'll discuss this important corporate attribute in more depth below.

 To help you decide which business form is best for you and for information and instructions for forming sole proprietorships, limited partnerships and corporations, see the listing of Nolo's business books and software in the Introduction.

# 1. Partnerships Versus Small Corporations

Most small, shared-ownership businesses prefer to start by forming a partnership, avoiding the extra time and expense required to form a corporation. Later, once the business becomes established and profitable, incorporation may make sense for tax, liability or employee benefits considerations as descussed further below. But in the beginning, the corporate form usually does not provide any extra benefits or incentives over the simpler, more easily managed partnership form.

Let's examine the main advantages and attributes commonly associated with incorporating and see if they hold up for the small, shared-ownership business.

## a. Limited Liability

As mentioned above, shareholders of a corporation are not normally liable for corporate debts or liability stemming from lawsuits or other business claim, while partners have open-ended personal liability for all partnership debts. However, for many small businesses, the difference between limited and unlimited liability is less significant than many people believe. Why?

Because in practice, limited liability rarely comes into play. To understand why, start by realizing that there are two important forms of potential debt problems a typical business must worry about: lawsuits and the inability to pay bills.

To deal with the first problem, most small businesses, whether incorporated or not, purchase insurance to protect them from the most obvious sorts of liability claims (such as insurance protecting restaurant owners from claims filed by customers who become ill or fall down in the premises). A corporation's limited liability status is obviously no substitute for business liability insurance, since limited liability doesn't protect the assets of the corporation from being wiped out by a successful claim.

 **If Insurance Isn't Available**   Limited liability can be a valuable protection if a small business is engaged in a high risk activity that may generate many damage claims and lawsuits, and where insurance coverage is unavailable or too expensive. In these situations, a business may wish to begin operations as a corporation.

But what about garden variety debts and bills? If the business loses money, as lots of new ventures do, doesn't limited liability protect individual shareholders from having personal assets taken as part of a corporate bankruptcy or liquidation? Again, yes in legal theory, but here too, limited liability protection is likely to be far less valuable than it first appears. Why? Because all lenders and most major creditors are so well aware of the rules of limited shareholder liability for corporate debts that it has become a matter of routine practice to require the owners of a new small business (whether incorporated or not) to personally guarantee any loan or significant extension of credit. By doing this, the corporate owners put themselves on much the same legal footing, vis-a-vis their creditors, as if they ran their business as a partnership.

**Exception**   We should note that providers of routine business and other supplies and services involving small amounts of money do not require a personal guarantee from corporate owners. In these situations, shareholders of an incorporated business can escape personal liability for these business debts if the corporation becomes insolvent.

**SOME CORPORATIONS MAY NOT QUALIFY FOR LIMITED LIABILITY**

In special circumstances, a court may hold individual shareholders personally responsible for all corporate debts, whether they personally guaranteed them or not. Lawyers call this "piercing the corporate veil." While this is the exception, not the rule, it can occur, particularly where an undercapitalized corporation acts unfairly or fraudulently towards creditors and does not pay attention to the formalities of corporate life (by issuing stock, holding regular meetings and keeping personal funds separate from corporate funds).

## b. Business Continuity

In theory, corporations have a perpetual legal existence. This means that if one (or even all) of the principal owners of a small corporation dies, the corporate entity continues to exist. Partnerships, on the other hand, theoretically dissolve when any one partner withdraws or dies.

Again, this advantage is mostly theoretical rather than real for the smaller business. In any small business, if one or more of the owners leaves, it may not be able to continue to operate (whether or not its legal existence remains intact). Besides, in partnerships with three or more partners, it's easy, and fully legal, to insert a standard clause in the partnership agreement that provides that the partnership entity continues to exist after one owner leaves or dies. And even with a two-person partnership that legally ends when one of the partners leaves the partnership, its easy to keep operating the business as a sole proprietorship.

The point is, no matter what business organization you choose, you need to think about what will happen if one of the owners quits or dies. Typically, you'll want to compensate a departing owner (or her inheritors) fairly for her interest and also want to preserve the business for the remaining owners. Among the questions you'll want to answer are: How is the value of that departing interest to be calculated? How can the remaining owners be assured they'll have adequate cash to buy out a departing owner? You don't avoid any of these issues and questions by choosing either a partnership or a corporation.

**NOTE**  When a corporation is ended and appreciated property is distributed to shareholders, the gain in value may be taxed both to the corporation and its shareholders. This means that it can potentially be more expensive from a tax point of view to close down a profitable corporation than a partnership.

**THE CORPORATE FORM CAN HELP RAISE CAPITAL**

For larger businesses that plan to raise money from outside investors, it can be easier to raise capital by selling corporate stock than by trying to sell participation in a partnership to passive investors (by setting up a limited partnership—see Section D, below). However, selling shares to the public is a complicated and costly procedure, best undertaken by larger firms with substantial prospects for profitability.

## c. Transferability of Ownership

In legal theory, corporate ownership in the form of stock can be transferred to new owners. By contrast, a partner's interest cannot be transferred without the consent of all partners unless, as is rarely the case, the partnership agreement expressly allows for free transferability. But again, normal business practice typically negates this difference. Why? Two reasons. First, the stock of most small corporations is extremely difficult, or even impossible, to sell since there is no regular market where they can be bought and sold. Even if the business is doing well, a potential buyer will almost always be more interested in purchasing the entire business or profitable business assets (for example, a building, patent invention, inventory, etc.) than one owner's corporate shares.

Second, recognizing that in any small business much depends on the efforts, skills and compatibility of a few people, the bylaws of many small corporations (as well as the partnership agreements of most partnerships) restrict the right of any owner to sell her interest to a third person, and provide that the remaining owners have the option to buy out the interest of any departing owner. So again, the realities of running a small business dictate that certain similar steps be taken to limit the transferability of interests in the enterprise to outside buyers, no matter what the legal form of the business.

## d. Business Formality

Some people say that the corporate form affords a certain built-in formality that other business organization don't possess. We don't think so. In an era where there are countless numbers of small corporations, adding "corp." to your name is unlikely to mean others will take your business more seriously. In reality, other businesses and creditors want to look at your balance sheet, not your corporate records book, to determine if you are an established business organization.

Besides, corporate formalities come with a price tag. Increased fees and paperwork are required to create a corporation. Indeed, filing the initial incorporation papers costs $300-$1,000 and up in some states (in California, the cost is a $100 filing fee and an initial, non refundable minimum franchise tax payment of $800). Moreover, a corporation requires more complicated and more costly tax filings and the preparation of ongoing corporate minute forms to document regular and special meetings of the board of directors and the shareholders. By contrast, a partnership is started with no state formalities and extra filing fees. Ongoing meetings can be held informally without the partners having to wear separate management (director) and ownership (shareholder) hats.

## e. Taxation

A partnership is not taxed. Partnership net income is only reported by, and taxed on, the individual partners' income tax returns. By contrast, a corporation must pay taxes on corporate profits and, in turn, shareholders must pay taxes on any dividend income they receive.

Does this mean a partnership enjoys an advantage over corporations because corporate profits are taxed twice while partnership income is only taxed once? For small businesses, this distinction usually is immaterial. Small corporations can avoid double taxation in two ways.

First, they can pay out to owners most of what would otherwise be corporate profits in the form of tax-deductible salaries and bonuses (rather than in dividends which are taxed both at the corporate and personal level). This is usually easy to do because the principal corporate employees are normally also the owners. As long as the owners actually work in the business and the salaries aren't outrageously unreasonable, paying the owners salaries as employees is acceptable to the IRS. Because monies paid in salaries, bonuses, social security, health plans and other fringe benefits are tax-deductible business expenses for the corporation, these expenses are not taxed at the corporate level.

Second, most small corporations have the option to elect federal "S" corporation tax status with the IRS (and, in many cases, with the state). An S corporation functions like a partnership for income tax purposes. Thus, an S corporation doesn't pay income taxes on profits, only the shareholders do. You may ask, "Why form an S corporation if you can attain the same tax results with a partnership?" The answer is that sometimes people desire one of the other attributes of incorporation, such as limited liability. Also, with S corporation status, individuals can, within limits and subject to other qualifications, apply losses from an active business against other income on their individual returns. This can be important if you expect a new business to lose money in its first years.

**TAX SAVINGS ARE POSSIBLE FOR SOME SMALL CORPORATIONS**
The corporate form can allow small business people who work for (as well as own) the corporation to pay less tax than if they were partners. This occurs in situations when a portion of corporate profits are retained in the corporation from one year to the next. The individual shareholder owner is taxed only on income she receives, whether paid to her in the form of corporate salary or as profits. The profits retained by the corporation are also taxed, but at a generally lower rate than individual income tax rates. Corporate profits are taxed at 15% for the first $50,000 and 25% on the next $25,000. In a partnership, these retained profits would be taxed as income to the partners at their marginal rate, which is likely to be 28%, or even 31% or more, whether or not cash was in fact distributed to them. For businesses that will pay all profits to owner-employees in the form of salaries and benefits, these initial low rates of corporate taxation offer no advantage. However, if yours is the type of business for which it's necessary to retain earnings for future operations, incorporating may in fact save you tax dollars.

## f. Putting It All Together

For most people who are planning a small shared-ownership business, there are few real-world advantages to incorporating instead of forming a partnership, at least at the start. Forming a partnership is usually easier and cheaper and is the logical choice as long as you take the time to prepare a well thought out partnership agreement. Therefore, we personally prefer to use the partnership form when starting most shared-ownership small businesses. As the business grows, it often makes good sense to convert to a corporation for tax and sometimes limited liability advantages. Fortunately, you can transform your partnership into a corporation whenever your partners agree to make this change.

# D. Limited Partnerships

A limited partnership is a legal entity that combines attributes of a partner-ship and a corporation. Although most commonly used to purchase and sell real estate, a limited partnership provides a way for business owners to raise money without having to take in new partners or form a corporation.

A limited partnership must have at least one entity or individual, called the "general partner," who runs things. This general partner can be another partnership, a corporation or a single human being. There can also be more than one general partner. However many there are, the general partner has the rights and potential liabilities normally involved in any partnership—such as management powers for the business and personal liability for busi-ness losses or debts. Limited partners, on the other hand, have no manage-ment powers, but neither are they personally liable for the debts of the partnership.

Limited partners are basically investors. The return they receive for their investment is defined in the limited partnership agreement. Sometimes, limited partners receive a set return on their investment. For instance, they might receive 10% interest annually, with principal, to be repaid in three installments over seven years. More commonly, limited partners are given the opportunity to receive a percentage of the profits (assuming the venture makes money) for a specific period of months or years or even forever. If the business fails, the most that the limited partners can lose is their investment (the amount of money or the property they contributed for their interest in the business).

Forming a limited partnership is more complicated and costly than forming a regular partnership. In many ways, establishing one is more like forming a corporation. Interests in limited partnerships are treated much the same as shares of corporate stock—security laws must be complied with before offering and selling these interests to investors. In addition, a certificate of limited partnership (similar to articles of incorporation) must be filed with the secretary of department of state and initial filing fees must be paid.[1]

 To help you decide which business form is best for you and for information and instructions for forming sole proprietorships, limited partnerships and corporations, see the listing of Nolo's business books and software in the Introduction.

# E. Partnerships

Below we discuss some of the key issues of partnership law to help you understand how partnerships are defined and regulated under state law and treated by the courts and the IRS.

## 1. What Is a Partnership?

The legal definition of a partnership is "an association of two or more persons to carry on as co-owners of a business for profit."

A person's intention to be a partner can be based upon an oral or written agreement or can be implied from the circumstances of a business operation. For example, if three people who have no other business relationship each inherit one-third of some real estate or a business, they don't automatically become partners, because they've never agreed to do business together. But if they then proceed to run the business or develop the land together, a court will consider them partners even if there is no written partnership agreement.

In general, receipt by a person of a share of the profits of an (unincorporated) business indicates that person is a partner in the business.

---

[1]In most states, the basic rules that govern the formation and operation of limited partnerships are contained in the state's Uniform Limited Partnership Act or Revised Uniform Limited Partnership Act.

**JOINT VENTURES (PARTNERSHIPS FOR A SINGLE PURPOSE)**

A joint venture (from "joint (ad)venture," a concept often used in the days of sailing vessels) is simply a partnership for a limited or specified purpose. If you and Jose go into the construction business together, that's a partnership. If you and Jose agree to build one house together, that's normally a joint venture. Common examples of joint ventures are natural resource projects—drilling for oil, or a cooperative mining venture.

Joint ventures are governed by partnership law. The relations of the joint venturers should be defined in an agreement, just like any partnership. Indeed, except for the fact that the agreement should state that the venture is a specifically defined one limited to a specified project, the same issues and problems must be resolved when creating a joint venture agreement as in a partnership agreement.

## 2. What Law Governs Partnerships?

Partnerships are governed by state law. The Uniform Partnership Act (or UPA) has been adopted (often with some slight modifications) in all states except Louisiana and contains the statutory rules that govern partnerships within the state.[2] Some of these statutory rules cannot be varied.

**EXAMPLE**   The UPA states that "Each partner is responsible for all debts of the partnership." You can't change this rule in your partnership agreement.

Other UPA rules only apply if the partners have not stated their own rule in their partnership agreement.

**EXAMPLE**   You can decide to split the profits and losses of your partnerships among your partners in any way you see fit. But if you don't specify a rule on this in your partnership agreement, then the UPA says that profits and losses must be split equally among the partners.

---

[2]In the Appendix, we list the legal citation to each state's UPA—where you can find it in your state's lawbooks.

**For Louisiana Partnerships**    Even though the UPA has not been adopted in your state, the clauses in *Partnership Maker* can still be used to create a sound partnership agreement. These *Partnership Maker* clauses are not tied specifically to the UPA—rather, they cover basic organizational and operational issues (division of contributions, profits, losses, voting power, etc.) which should be discussed and agreed to by the partners of any partnership prior to doing business together.

## 3. Partnership Purposes

Partnerships can be organized for all sorts of purposes. They can sell products or services just as they can manufacture, mine or operate as agents.

## 4. Equal Versus Unequal Ownership

Partners don't have to share ownership equally. You can agree on any percentage of individual ownership or distribution of the profits that you want. Thus, one partner could own 80% of the partnership and four more could own 5% each.

## 5. Compensation of Partners

Partners normally don't receive salaries; instead, they periodically divide a percentage of the profits of the business. However, especially in situations where partners need regular incomes, it's common for partners to take on an agreed-upon amount from the business—known as a draw—at regular intervals (for example, monthly, biweekly) against their yearly partnership shares.

# 6. Powers of the Partners

Each partner has full power to represent and bind the partnership within the normal course of business. This makes it obvious why trust is so vital in a partnership. One partner can obligate the other partners, even if they never authorized him to do so. Indeed, in many circumstances, a partner can bind a partnership even when the other partners told him not to.

**EXAMPLE**   Al, Fred and Mike are partners in a printing business. They discuss buying an expensive new press and vote two-to-one against it. Fred, the disgruntled loser, goes out and signs a contract for the press with a company that has no knowledge of Al's and Mike's vehement opposition. Since this is within the normal course of business, Fred's act binds the partnership.

It is legal to limit the powers of any partner in the partnership agreement. However, those limits won't be binding on people outside the partnership who have no actual knowledge of them. Legally, outsiders are entitled to rely on the apparent authority of a partner, as determined by the customs of the particular trade or business involved. When Fred bought the printing press, the salesman—as long as he had no actual knowledge of the partnership's limits on Fred—relied on his apparent authority (a partner of a printing business can reasonably be expected to have the authority to buy a press). If Fred sought to bind the printing partnership in a deal to open a chain of massage parlors, an outsider probably wouldn't be able to rely on his signature alone as binding on the partnership.

## SOME WORDS OF ENCOURAGEMENT

We recite these rules of partnership responsibility not to discourage you from entering into a partnership, but to alert you to the fact that, like any human endeavor, there are risks to be acknowledged and dealt with. By the use of insurance and other common sense business practices, many of the potential partnership risks can be minimized. And of course, no matter how you organize your small business, one thing is paramount: deal only with people you know to be completely honest. The fact that there are so many functioning partnerships in the United States is probably the best evidence that it's possible to do all of these things.

## 7. Legal Responsibilty of Partners

Partners owe complete loyalty to the partnership and cannot engage in any activity which conflicts with the partnership's business. They must also act in good faith when dealing with one another.

Here are the essential honest business rules that the courts have said apply to each partner:

- A partner cannot secretly obtain for herself an opportunity available to the partnership.

- Each partner must disclose any and all material facts affecting the business to the other partners.

- Partnership assets cannot be diverted for personal use.

- Partners cannot fail to distribute partnership profits to other members of the partnership.

## 8. Liability

As we've said, partners are personally and individually liable for all the legal obligations of the partnership. Another related legal principle is that each partner is personally liable for all partnership debts that cannot be paid by the partnership. Partners are not, however, liable for the personal, non-pertnership debts and obligations of another partner.[3]

Partners are also liable for any money damages that result from the negligence of another partner, as well as damages that result from any frauds or other intentional acts done in the ordinary course of partnership business.

---

[3]If one partner is having financial problems outside the partnership, the partner's creditors can seek to get at her share of the partnership business. This can result in obvious problems and disrupt the business of the partnership.

## 9. Partnership Taxation

Partnerships are not liable for federal or state income taxes. An informational partnership tax return must be filed once a year. Any profits or losses from the partnership flow through the partnership to the individual partners.

## 10.   Partnerships and Paperwork

The technicalities of establishing and maintaining a small business partnership are fairly easy to accomplish. Most of your energy should go into preparing a sound partnership agreement that fairly reflects the aspirations, expectations, rights, responsibilities and, yes, worries of all partners. This agreement is private and is not filed with any governmental bureau, department or agency.

All partnerships must file Form SS-4 with the IRS to obtain a taxpayer I.D. number. Also, if the partnership operates under a fictitious name (a name other than those of the partners), it must file a fictitious business name statement with the county clerk, secretary of state or a similar county or state agency.

**EXAMPLE**    If Wang, Olivier and Simmons call themselves Ace Electric, they'll have to file a fictitious business name statement for this fictitious business name.

And, of course, partnerships must comply with the same small business and tax paperwork requirements common to any other business. This includes getting a business license, a sales tax resale permit if goods will be sold, filing payroll and unemployment tax returns if there are employees, and generally dealing with all the rest of the bureaucratic procedures that go with starting operating a business. And, of course, there's the internal recordkeeping, including sales, accounts, receivable, general ledger and other accounting records, which are required of any business.

# PARTNERSHIP AGREEMENT CLAUSES

I n this chapter we cover all the partnership agreement clauses contained in the program. Clauses are numbered and discussed below in the order they appear on the Main Screen of the program.

The material here repeats some of the help text for the clauses and fields (blanks) within clauses shown on the screens in the program. It also contains additional information and examples for a number of central partnership areas, such as choosing a name, selecting a buy-out clause and arriving at the best valuation method for partnership interests.

Here's how we suggest you use this material: First, skim through this chapter once. Then run the program and read the help text for each clause as you prepare a first draft of your partnership agreement. Then, for additional information on a clause, return here. Once your first draft is complete, share it with your partner or partners along with these materials. Leave plenty of time to discuss important issues. Once tentative agreements are reached on these issues, load your agreement back into the program and create a second draft by making changes to your original responses, adding or removing clauses, etc. (as explained in Chapter 1). This may be all you need, but chances are at least as good that you'll want to produce several drafts of your agreement before all of the clauses in it are acceptable to all partners.

**Remember**    If you are confused by any of the clauses or wish to customize the legal language to suit the specific needs of your partnership, you may wish to consult a lawyer before producing and printing your final agreement.

**To Save Time and Work**    The distribution disk contains a partnership agreement titled SAMPLE.DOC. This agreement contains the clauses marked as "suggested" in the program —those covering basic partnership matters that we suggest all partnerships use. In cases where alternative clauses are available to cover one of these matters (such as the buy-out valuation method), we have chosen the clause most suitable for beginning or smaller partnerships. Simply load this agreement into the program, add or remove any clauses that you wish, then fill in the blanks to create a first draft of our partnership agreement. A listing of the clauses included in the SAMPLE.DOC agreement is included in the Appendix.

**To See All Partnership Clauses**     For easy reference, we have also included a printout of all partnership clauses contained in the program in the Appendix.

**USE OF HIS OR HER IN PARTNERSHIP CLAUSES**
In some partnership agreement clauses, individual partners are identified as "he or she." We suggest that it's wise to leave the phrase "he or she" in your agreement rather than edit the clause to eliminate the reference to one sex. After all, it's hard to be absolutely sure you'll never take in a partner of the other sex. And leaving the clause reading "he or she' won't cause any harm if all partners are the same sex.

# Preliminary Clauses

The first category of clauses shown on the main program screen includes clauses that are customarily placed at the beginning of a partnership agreement (the name of the partnership, its term, and the purposes and goals of the partnership, etc.).

# Name Clauses

The three name clauses below, clauses 1 through 3, should be included in all partnership agreements.

■

The first clause specifies the names of the partners and the effective date of your agreement, as follows:

## Clause 1. Names of Partners and Effective Date

*This partnership agreement is entered into and effective as of*

_____, *by:*

*Names of Partners*

_____

_____


**Effective Date**    Unless you specify otherwise, the effective date of your agreement is the date it is signed by your partners. For most users this is fine. To show this, fill in this field with the words "the date of signing of this agreement." Or, if the agreement will be signed by different partners on different dates, you should insert the words "the date the last partner signs this agreement."

If you do wish to specify a particular date here (for example, January 1, 1992) as the effective date of your agreement, you are free to do so. If you take this approach, make sure that the date specified is on or after the date the last partner signs the printed agreement.

**Names of the Partners**    Show the names of the partners, with one partner name typed in each field (blank). The list for the partners' names (as with all program lists), contains two fields initially. If there are more than two partners, you can add additional names to the list. First press <Enter> to add the clause to your agreement, then press <Esc> to return to the clause panel. Next, use the arrow key to highlight one of the fields in the list, choose the Field command in the menu bar and select Add (press the </> key, then <F>, then <A> or use the arrow keys). Each time you do this, a blank field is added to the bottom of the list for you to insert the name of another partner.

## Clause 2. Name of the Partnership

*The name of the partnership is*

_____.

The partnership name given here is often the last names of the partners, for example "Smith, Weiss and Fong." However, this isn't mandatory. The partnership can be given a more imaginative or fictional name, such as "The Merry Mongoose." If you do choose a fictitious partnership name, that is one which does not use the names of the partners, see the discussion under clause 3 below on making sure you have a right to use that name.

## Clause 3. Name of the Business

*The name of the partnership business is*

_____.

The business name given here is the name you will actually use to carry on business. It can be, and often is, the same as the name of the partnership given in the clause 2. For example, both the business name and the partnership name can be "Smith, Weiss and Fong." But the business can also have a different name. You could decide to use just one partner's name, for example "Smith Lumber Co." Or, you can legally choose a fictitious name, such as "Two-by-Four Lumber." Again, a fictitious name is simply one that does not include the last names of your partners. There is nothing under-handed about using a fictitious name—many partnerships do it to identify their business in a more descriptive or imaginative way. If you do choose to use a fictitious business (or partnership) name, you're entering into an area where you can face serious problems if you choose a name already in use. So, let's take a closer look at how you can sensibly choose a business name.

## The Importance of Your Business Name

Your business names may turn out to be one of your most important business assets, as it can come to represent goodwill of your business. We don't mean this just in an accounting or tax sense, but primarily that the people and institutions you do business with will identify you mostly by your business name. For this reason, as well as a number of practical reasons, such as not wanting to print new stationery or checks, change promotional literature, create new logos, etc., you will want to thoughtfully select a name you'll be happy with for a long time.

Finding an appropriate and available name for your business can require patience. It's often best not to act on your first impulse—try a few names and ask others for feedback.

 **Don't Use a Corporate Designator in Your Name**    A partnership cannot legally hold itself out to be a corporation. This means that you can't use Inc., Ltd., Corporation, Incorporated, Limited (or in some states, Company or Co.) in or after your name. However, terms that don't directly imply that you're incorporated, such as Associates, Affiliates, Group and Organization, are normally okay.

## Checking on the Legal Availability of a Name

Whatever name you decide to use (even your own), it's prudent to check to be sure another business isn't already using that name, or one confusingly similar. This matter isn't, unfortunately, just legal nit-picking. Business names can be, and often are, legally protected trademarks, or service marks. This means that a business with the prior claim to a name identical or similar to yours can sue to enjoin (stop) you from using your name or can force you to change it. Money damages may be awarded by the court for lost sales or loss of goodwill suffered by the name's rightful owner due to your use of the name. If you violate a trademark or service mark registered with the U.S. Patent and Trademark Office, treble damages (three times the actual money damages suffered as a result of the infringement), defendant's profits and court costs may be awarded, and the goods with the offending labels or marks may be ordered to be confiscated and destroyed.

Checking on the availability of a name can take some work. One partial short-cut can be to geographically limit your name, adding a particular limitation, such as "of Georgia" or "in Northern Wyoming" or "in downtown Los Angeles." Thus, if you call yourself Southern Oregon Lumber, and you are the only one, you should be okay. But even here, it pays to check. If there is an Oregon Lumber Co., and they operate in southern Oregon, they might object that your name is confusingly similar.

Without discussing the intricacies of federal and state trademark, service mark and tradename law, the basic rule is that the ultimate right to use a particular name will usually be decided on the basis of who was first to actually use the name in connection with a particular trade business, activity, service or product. In deciding who has the right to a name in case of a conflict, the similarity of the types of businesses or organizations and their geographical proximity are often taken into account. The more local your business (for example, a gardening service or house painting business), the less you have to worry about. But even at the village square level, you can run into problems if you don't take care. For example, Benjamin and Jerry Fisher would very likely hear from the lawyers of another Ben & Jerry if they put their first names on an ice cream shop. However, if they open Ben & Jerry's Plumbing, the fact that fixing pipes couldn't be confused with making or selling ice cream should mean their name was legally okay, at least as far as the famous Ben & Jerry's went. But they should still check to be sure no other Ben & Jerry used that name or anything similar (B & J, for instance) in their area, or that no national plumbing franchise uses it.

Below we suggest some name-checking procedures you may wish to use to be more confident of the uniqueness of your business name:

**Check State Trademarks and Service Marks**   Call the trademark section of your secretary of state's office and ask if your proposed name is the same or similar to trademarks and service marks registered with the state (some offices may ask for a written request and a small fee before performing this search).

**Check State and County Assumed Business Name Files**   Your secretary of state should also be able to indicate whether assumed or fictitious names are registered statewide with the secretary's office, locally (at the county level) with the county clerk, or both. If names are registered at the state level, call the assumed name section at the secretary of state's office and ask if your proposed name is the same or similar to a registered assumed or fictitious name. Also call your local county clerk's office to ask how you can check assumed business name filings. In most states, assumed or fictitious business name statements, or "doing business as" (dba) statements, are filed with the county clerk's office. In most cases, you will have to go in and check the assumed business name files in person. It takes just a few minutes to do this.

**Check Directories**   Check major metropolitan phone book listings, business and trade directories, etc., to see if another company or group is using a name similar to your proposed name. Larger public libraries keep phone directories for many major cities throughout the country, as well as trade directories.

**Check the Federal Trademark Register**   Go to a large public library or special business and government library in your area that carries the Federal Trademark Register. This consists of a listing of trademark and service mark names broken into categories of goods and services.

**Other Methods**   If yours is a local business and you haven't turned up any names close to the one you want to use in use by another business similar to yours, you have likely done enough investigation. However, if yours is a big business, or one that hopes to operate across state lines, you may wish to go further in your name search. To do this, you can pay a private records search company to check various databases and name listings. Alternatively, or in conjunction with your own efforts or search procedures, you can pay a trademark lawyer to oversee or undertake these searches for you (or to render a legal opinion if your search turns up a similar name).

**CHECKING YOUR NAME BY COMPUTER**

Most of the business name listings mentioned above, including Yellow Page listings and business director databases, as well as the federal and state trademark registers, are available as part of several commercial computer databases. For example, the federal and state registers can be accessed through the Trademarkscan service which is part of the Trademark Research Center forum (Go Traderc) on CompuServe database (call 1-800-848-8990 for subscription information) or the Dialog database (call 1-800-462-3411). If you own or have access to a computer and a modem, and are already signed up on one of these databases, you can check your proposed name against the names in the federal and state registers in just a few minutes time (for an extra charge for your time while using the Trademarkscan service).

## Protecting Your Name

Once you've decided on a fictitious name that you have concluded is free for you to use, you may want to take steps to protect your name from subsequent use by other businesses. For example, if your name is used to identify your products or services, you may wish to register it with your secretary of state and with the United States Patent and Trademark Office as a trademark or service mark. Registration in other states may also be appropriate if you plan to conduct operations there.

Federal registration costs $200 and can be accomplished on one of two grounds:

1. you have used the name in interstate commerce (that is, in two or more states) in connection with the marketing of goods or services; or

2. you intend to use the name in interstate commerce in connection with the marketing of goods or services.

If you specify the second reason in your trademark application, you must file an affidavit (sworn statement) within six months stating that the name has been placed in actual use. This costs an additional $100. Simply stated, this means it is possible to reserve ownership of a trademark before actually using it, but you have to pay at least $100 extra for the privilege.

**SUGGESTED READING**

*Trademark: How To Name Your Business & Product* by Elias & McGrath (Nolo Press) shows you how to obtain a trademark, step-by-step. We strongly recommend you study this book carefully if you have any questions about choosing or protecting your business name.

## Filing a Fictitious Name Statement

If you use any or all of the partners' last names, you do not have to register the business name with any government agency (as mentioned, it may be a good idea to file trademark registrations). But if you use a different (in legal lingo, "fictitious") business name, state law or local ordinances normally require you to register that name. Happily, this is neither a complicated nor particularly expensive procedure. Registration involves filing a single statement, often colloquially referred to as a dba (doing business as statement), and, in many states, publishing a series of brief notices in a local newspaper—those meaningless small print announcements we all see and ignore. Contact your city or county clerk, or tax and license officer, for more information.

# Term of the Partnership

The clauses here are optional. Include either clause 4 or 5 in your agreement.

Clause 4 states the normal rule that most partnerships use. It indicates that the partnership will last indefinitely (until it is dissolved).

### Clause 4. Term—Until Dissolution of Partnership

*The partnership shall last until it is dissolved by all the partners or according to the terms of this agreement.*

■

Sometimes partners decide they don't want an open-ended agreement. This is particularly true in joint ventures (partnerships for a specific limited purpose or project). The following alternative clause allows you to limit the term of the partnership to a specific date or event:

---

### Clause 5. Term—Until Specific Date or Event

*The partnership shall commence as of the date of this agreement and shall continue until   [specify an event or date, such as "the sale of 126 Venture Street, Albany, New York"]  , at which time it shall be dissolved and its affairs wound up.*

---

## Purposes and Goals of the Partnership

The following clause should be included in all partnership agreements to show the purposes of the partnership:

---

### Clause 6. Purposes of the Partnership

*The purposes of the partnership are:   [insert a short statement of purposes]  .*

Generally, it's wise to state the purpose broadly, to allow for possible expansion for the business.

**EXAMPLE**    Three partners plan to start a consulting business to provide specialized advice on the employment problems of county governments in Colorado. At first, they decide to call the business, "Colorado County Government Consulting Service." Then they ask themselves what happens if they prosper. Perhaps the next step would be to do consulting for governmental entities generally, or for a mix of governmental and private clients in fields other than employment and outside Colorado. After considerable discussion, they decide to call their partnership "Expert Consultants" and to define the business purposes here as "consulting in the public and private sectors," leaving out limiting or qualifying words like "employment," "county governments" and "Colorado."

Another way to deal with the same problem would be to include both definitions as to the scope of the business. That is to say you might insert a longer statement similar to the following:

> *The purposes of the partnership are:* <u>*The original purpose of our partnership business is to provide high quality consulting services to county governments in the State of Colorado concerning employee relations. However, it is also contemplated that in the future, general consulting services may be offered to governmental and private business units at all levels within and without Colorado.*</u>

There's no specific language we can provide that will be helpful in drafting your purpose clause. It all depends on the nature of your business and your future plans. State what you want to do in everyday, plain English, leaving plenty of wriggle room for future changes, and you'll be fine.

**A Narrow Purpose Clause Can Eliminate Conflicts of Interest**    A few partnerships don't want a broad purpose clause. For instance, if you're engaged in a limited enterprise, such as a joint venture, it's likely you will want to limit your business to this, particularly if it's contemplated that a partner will also work in a closely related business. In such cases, you'll not only want to narrowly define the partnership business, but also specifically exclude that type of outside work from your purposes to prevent possible conflict-of-interest problems. (See Outside Activities by Partners, clauses 42 through 44 below for specific clauses related to outside business activities by partners).

■

Some partners also wish to express the personal goals, wishes and intentions of the partners in their partnership agreement. Here's the optional clause to include to do this:

## Clause 7. Goals of the Partnership

*The goals and dreams of each partner are set out below. The partners understand that this statement is not legally binding, but include it in the partnership agreement as a record of their hopes and intentions:*
*_____[recital of goals ]_____.*

**GOALS EXAMPLE**
*Danielle and Li-Shan have each worked making women's clothing. They've decided to combine their skills and energies and open a women's clothing store selling handmade clothes. Danielle and Li-Shan hope to make a very comfortable living. However, Li-Shan wants it on record that she does not want to sacrifice her weekends and vacations to the job. Both partners understand that this clause is an expression of intention and is not legally binding.*

# Contribution Clauses

The clauses in this category deal with contributions of money, property or services by the partners to the partnership. Clause 8, the basic contributions clause, should be included in all partnership agreements. The remaining eight contribution clauses (clauses 9 through 16) are optional.

Here's the basic contributions clause that describes the partners' contributions, sets the percentage of ownership of each partner, and specifies the date for the payment of contributions to the partnership:

## Clause 8. Contributions

*The following persons shall make the following contributions of cash property or services to the partnership in return for the following ownership shares in the partnership:*

| *Names of Partners* | *Description of Contributions* | *Percentages* |
|---|---|---|
| _____ | _____ | _____ |
| _____ | _____ | _____ |

*Except as may otherwise be provided above for a particular contribution, contributions shall be paid in full or transferred and delivered to the partnership on or before  [date of payment] .*

### CAPITAL ACCOUNT

The term "capital account" is one you will encounter often in your partnership business. Simply stated, a partner's capital account is the dollar value of her ownership interest in the business. Another way of phrasing this is that a capital account reflects a partner's total equity in the business.

Example: Merv and Hayden start a business booking night-club comedians. Each contributes $40,000 cash. Thus each partner's capital account is $40,000. Now suppose the business loses a net $10,000 the first year, or $5,000 a partner. Each partner's capital account will now be $35,000.

Determining the worth of a partner's capital account can be far more complex if, for instance, the partnership owns appreciated property or inventory. Once a business is underway, it often requires an accountant to determine the current value of a capital account.

Normally, the percentages shown in the third column will be the same as each partner's percentage of contribution to the partnership. For example, if two partners contribute $10,000, each will normally be given a 50% share in the third column here. This isn't required, however, and occasionally there may be a good reason to give a partner a bigger or smaller share than would be indicated by the amount of their contribution. In the discussion below, we look at different contribution considerations and scenarios and examine different types of payment.

## Contributions of Cash

Frequently, each partner contributes cash to get a new business started. A key decision here is whether each partner contributes an equal amount. If this is possible, we think it's desirable; otherwise, the partners who contribute the most cash may want more than an equal say in management decisions.

**CASH EXAMPLE**    If three partners will make equal cash contributions totaling $15,000, insert $5,000 as the description of the contribution for each partner.

**Unequal Cash Contributions**    Sometimes partners simply can't afford to contribute the same amount of cash. There are many ways to handle the problems inherent in this disparity. One is to have the partner with more money to contribute cut back her contribution to the amount put up by the other partner and advance the rest of the money in the form of a loan. Or if a person will contribute more work than others, you can pay this person a salary for the extra work, rather than treating these additional services as a capital contribution.

Another solution is to have the partner who contributes less cash contribute more services, valued at a set hourly rate, until the contributions made by the partners are equalized.

 **Unequal Contributions Can Lead to Problems**    If there's a significant disparity between work and money contributed by different partners, there's a real potential for conflict. The person who contributes the most of either may come to resent the others, especially if the business gets off to a slow start.

At the very least, you need to recognize that unequal contributions can cause problems, and talk out what's mutually comfortable—or at least acceptable—to resolve it.

## Deferred Cash Contributions

If a partner cannot initially contribute the desired amount of cash, one method for handling this is for her to make deferred contributions—in other words, payments over time. These deferred payments can be arranged any way you decide, including equal monthly installments or payments from business profits. Describe any deferred contribution arrangement in your description of the contribution in clause 8.

### DEFERRED CASH EXAMPLES

"Partner A shall make a contribution to the partnership of $X per month, beginning January 1, 2001, until he or she has contributed the sum of $10,000."

"Partner B shall contribute to the partnership 10% of his or her share of the partnership profits for each fiscal year, beginning January 1, 19__, until he or she has contributed the amount of $10,000."

## Contributions of Property

It's common that one, some, or even all, partners contribute property as well as, or instead of, cash to a partnership. This property can be real property (real estate) or personal property (everything else). Also, a partner can sell or lease personal or real property to a partnership. Obviously, property contribution scenarios can range from the simple to the exceedingly complex. In your description of the contribution in clause 8, you should briefly describe the property, its value and the conditions, if any, placed on its transfer to the partnership and its use by it. If the property is difficult to describe, describe it in detail on a separate sheet of paper marked "Exhibit A" and insert the following phrase in the description of contribution field:

## PROPERTY EXAMPLES

"Real property known as __[street address ]__ and more particularly described in Exhibit A, attached to this agreement, market value $_____."

"1989 Ford pickup truck; market value: $8,000."

 **TAX NOTE**   Be sure to examine carefully the tax consequences of contributions of property, especially real property that has appreciated in value. For example, if a partner transfers appreciated property to a partnership (whose value is greater than the amount the partner originally paid for it) and the partnership sells the property, a taxable gain will result. You will want to make sure that this gain is allocated properly.

## Contributions of Services

One or more of the partners often receive an ownership interest in the business at least in part because of a promise to contribute personal services to the business. If a partner is to contribute services to the partnership, make sure to specify the amount and/or value of services that the partner will perform in the description of contribution column of contribution clause 8.

**EXAMPLE**   Elsa and Daphne form a partnership owned 50% by each to cater parties. Each will spend equal time on food preparation and service. Elsa contributes $10,000 to get the business going. Daphne agrees to contribute unpaid labor as a bookkeeper and business manager for nine months over and above the time she spends on parties, instead of contributing cash, which she doesn't have. A description of Daphne's future services is included in the description of contribution column for Daphne, as follows:

| Name of Partner | Description of Contribution | Percentage |
|---|---|---|
| Elsa | $10,000 | 50% |
| Daphne | Nine months future services as Bookkeeper and Business Manager valued at $10,000 | 50% |

# Interest on Contributed Capital

Clauses 9 and 10 below are optional; include one of these two clauses if you wish to cover the issue of whether partners are entitled to receive interest payments from the business on the capital they contribute to get it started.

Usually, most partnerships decide not to pay interest in contributions. Why pay money to yourselves from your own business for the money you put in? If this is your decision, there is generally no need to mention the subject in your partnership agreement. However, if you have a reason for stating this prohibition explicitly in your agreement, here's the clause to use:

### Clause 9. No Interest Paid on Contributed Capital

*No partner shall be entitled to receive any interest on any capital contribution.*

■

In rare instances, partners will decide they want to pay interest on capital contributions. If interest is paid, many payment terms are possible. For example, you might specify that partners only receive interest in years where net profits exceed a specified percent, or that interest is optional and shall be decided upon yearly by the partners, etc. Here is the alternative clause that provides for payment of interest on capital contributions:

## Clause 10. Interest Paid on Contributed Capital

*Each partner shall be entitled to interest on his or her capital contribution accruing at the rate of _____ percent per year from the date the contribution is paid. This interest shall be treated as an expense to be charged against income on the partnership books and shall be paid to the partner entitled to it on the following terms:  [specify terms, for example, "quarterly" or "only upon termination of the partnership"].*

# Failure To Make Contributions

The four clauses in this group cover what happens if a partner fails to contribute the initial cash, property or service contributions required  by the partnership agreement (under clause 8)? You may ask why should we concern ourselves with this? After all, if we don't trust our partners to put up what they say they will, the partnership is doomed anyway. On the other hand, if for some reason one proves unwilling or unable to abide by his commitment, you'll probably be in better shape if you've provided in advance for what you want to do. Does the business break up or does the partnership continue without the defaulting partner? Are additional contributions required from the remaining partners?

If you wish to cover this issue, include either clause 11, 12 or 13 as your basic clause. Then, if relevant, add clause 14 to your agreement to specify a special rule for failures to contribute services to the partnership.

## Clause 11. Failure to Contribute—Partnership Dissolves

*Except as otherwise provided in this agreement, if any partner fails to pay his or her initial contribution to the partnership by the date required by this agreement, the partnership shall immediately dissolve and each partner who has paid all or any portion of his or her initial contribution to the partnership's capital shall be entitled to a return of the funds and properties he or she contributed.*

## Clause 12.  Failure to Contribute— No Additional Contributions Required

*Except as otherwise provided in this agreement, if any partner fails to pay his or her contribution to the partnership capital as required by this agreement, the partnership shall not dissolve or terminate, but it shall continue as a partnership of only the partners who have made their initial capital contributions as required and without any partner who has failed to do so. In that case, the share in the partnership's profits and losses allocated under this agreement to any partner who has failed to make his or her initial contribution shall be reallocated to the remaining partners in proportion to their respective shares of partnership profits and losses as specified in this agreement.*

## Clause 13. Failure to Contribute—Additional Contributions Required

*Except as otherwise provided in this agreement, if any partner fails to pay his or her initial contributions to the partnership's capital as required by this agreement, the partnership shall not dissolve or terminate, but shall continue as a partnership of the partners who have made their initial capital contributions and without any partner who shall have failed to do so, but only if the remaining partners pay the initial capital contribution that was to have been made by the non-contributing partner or partners. The partnership shall promptly give written notice of this failure to all partners who have made their initial capital contributions. The notice shall specify the amount not paid. Within _____ days after the notice is given, the remaining partners shall pay the amount of the defaulted contribution in proportion to the respective amount they are required to pay to the partnership's capital under this agreement. That share of the profits of the partnership belonging to non-contributing partners shall then be reallocated to the remaining partner in proportion to their respective shares of separate property profits and losses under this agreement.*

■

Add optional clause 14 below if you wish to specify a special rule for partners that fail to provide promised service contributions to the partnership. Service contributions can be more difficult to handle because they're made over time, not at once. What happens if a service partner quits on the first day? That's easy. He hasn't contributed anything, so he does not become a partner. But what happens if he quits after contributing 90% of what he promised? Or, as is more possible, suppose he doesn't quit, but regularly contributes only 70% or 90% of the hours he promises? These questions indicate one more type of problem you take on when you accept a service-contributing partner. Work out what you think is fair, then include the following clause in your agreement, filling in the terms for failures to contribute services to the partnership:

## Clause 14. Failure to Contribute Services

If _[name(s) of partners who will contribute services of fail(s)]_ fails to contribute the services as promised, the partnership shall proceed as follows: _[specify terms]_ .

# Future Contributions

We don't think it normally makes sense to insert language in your partnership agreement about what will happen in the future if your partnership business needs more money. Adopting a partnership provision to require future cash contributions makes even less sense. If a partner doesn't have the cash needed three years from now, what good is a clause you drafted long in advance? Nevertheless, despite our views, we know some people like the sense of commitment that required future contributions provide. If you really want to require future contributions, you're not prohibited from doing so. If you wish to cover this, include either clause 15 or 16 in your agreement.

Most smaller partnerships will wish to require a unanimous vote of partners to require future contributions. Legally, you can provide that future contributions are allowed by a less than unanimous vote—perhaps a simple majority, or two-thirds—of the partners. But in a small partnership, this isn't really feasible. If one partner can't—or won't—put up additional cash, it's likely to be destructive to try and bludgeon her into it. If you wish, you can edit this clause to add more detail, such as providing how notice of the need for increased capital is to be given, how much time the partners have to make the contributions, etc.

## Clause 15. Future Contributions—If Approved by Unanimous Vote

*If, at any future time, more money is required to carry on the partnership business, and all of partners vote to increase the capital contributions required by partners, the additional capital shall be paid in by the partners as follows: [specify the amount and terms for payment of future contributions] .*

■

Here is an alternative clause that requires annual contributions. We think such a clause is usually not warranted. It assumes that more money will be needed and that all partners will be willing and able to contribute it. In a business that will surely need more capital to expand, putting a portion of profits back into the business can make sense, but it's usually better to determine this at the end of each year, not at the beginning of the partnership.

## Clause 16. Future Contributions—Required Annually

*Each partner shall contribute annually [insert dollar amount or percentage of profits] to the partnership's capital for a period of _____ years.*

# Loans to the Partnership

As we said earlier in our discussion of contributions, sometimes partners simply can't afford to contribute the same amount of cash. There are many ways to handle the problems inherent in this disparity. One is to have what would otherwise be the excess cash contributed by one partner be converted to a loan. In other words, all partners make equal contributions, and one partner also loans money to the business.

**EXAMPLE** Naomi and Toni open a modern dance studio. They both contribute $20,000, and Naomi loans the business an additional $30,000 at 10% annual interest, to be repaid over three years.

The two loan clauses in this category are optional. Include either or both if they apply to you.

Here is the clause that can be included in your agreement to show a loan of cash to the partnership. You can edit the clause to add provisions to the loan clause if you agree on them, such as a payment schedule, security, etc.

## Clause 17. Cash Loan

_____*[name of partner]*_____ *shall loan the partnership* _*[amount]*_ *by* _*[date ]*_ . *The partnership shall pay* _____ *percent interest on the loan.*

■

A partner may loan specific items of property, such as tools or antiques or vehicles, to the partnership. Often, no fee is paid by the partnership for the use of the property (though you can provide for that if you decide to). You also need to decide when the items are to be returned. This could be when the partnership ends, when the loaning partner wants the property back, or after a set period of time, such as one year.

Here's the clause to use for loans of property:

### Clause 18. Loan of Property

> _[name of partner]_ will loan to the partnership the following item(s) of
> property: _[description of property]_ . Each item of property lent to the
> partnership shall remain the separate property of the lending partner and
> shall be returned to that partner on the following terms: _[insert whatever_
> _terms you've agreed on—for example, "upon dissolution of the_
> _partnership," or "upon demand," etc.]_

If the property is not simple to describe, you can add "as more particularly
described in Exhibit A, B, etc., attached to this agreement" and attach your
description to your printed agreement.

# Profits, Losses and Draws

Clearly you'll want to decide how partners will be paid from the profits of the
partnership. Realistically, you'll need to make a profit for any partners to get
paid. But after all, you're going into business to make money, so it makes
sense to think about what will happen when you do. The first issue here is
how you'll divide profits. Next is the timing of payments of profits to the
partners. You may also wish to decide on a general or specific limitation on
paying out all profits to partners in order to keep working capital on hand.
Finally you should consider whether partners may receive a draw against their
share of the profits—that is, whether one or more partners will be paid
sooner than the other partners.

## Profits and Losses

If your partnership agreement doesn't state how profits and losses are to be
divided, the Uniform Partnership Act provides that all partners share both
equally, even if they contributed unequal amounts of cash, property or labor
to the partnership. If the partnership agreement defines how profits are to be

distributed, but doesn't mention losses, the UPA states that each partner must contribute toward the losses according to his or her share of profits.[1] Obviously, if you want a different result, you'll need to include your intentions in your partnership agreement. But, even if profits and losses are to be shared equally, it's best to state this expressly in your partnership agreement, rather than rely on the UPA. This will minimize any possibility of later disagreement.

Some partnerships will choose to divide profits and losses unequally. This can be done for all sorts or reasons, such as one partner contributing more work or more money to the partnership. There's no formula that defines when you want to give one or more partner a larger or smaller share—it's your business and you can divide the profits and losses any way you all agree is fair.

Here is the clause you should include in your agreement to divide profits and losses among the partners. Note that initially the program shows each partner receiving a share of the profits and losses that are equal to the percentage of ownership figures for each partner as given in your contributions clause (clause 8). You may change these program supplied percentages to show any percentages you wish.

## Clause 19. Division of Profits and Losses

*The partnership profits and losses shall be shared among the partners as follows:*

| Name of Partner | % of Profits | % of Losses |
|---|---|---|
| _____ | _____ | _____ |
| _____ | _____ | _____ |

---

[1]UPA Section 18a.

■

The next consideration is when profits are to be paid. There is no absolute need to do this, but it often makes sense to set out a definite time for distribution of profits in your agreement. For example, you can specify that profits shall be distributed 30 days after the end of each fiscal year of the partnership, or 15 days after the end of each quarter. Once you decide on your formula, you can insert the terms in the following optional clause:

### Clause 20. Date for Distribution of Profits

*Profits of the partnership shall be distributed in cash to the partners, in proportion to their respective shares in the partnership's profits, in amounts equal to the partnership's net profit for that period, according to the following schedule:* _[insert schedule or other terms for payment of profits]_ .

## Restrictions on Payment of Profits

The next issue to consider is whether you wish to set limits on the payouts of profits to cover contingencies or provide for the future needs of the business. Obviously, most businesses won't last long if they don't plan for the future and keep a reserve against unexpected problems. You may wonder if there's a standard percentage of profits that are retained by a partnership business— for new equipment, expansions, employees' bonuses, whatever—before any remaining profits are distributed to the partners. It's a good question. But the answer is no; once again, there's no set formula. It's up to you to decide how prudent or daring you want to be.

We have included two alternative clauses in the program for setting limits on the payout of profits. Use of either of these clauses is optional.

Here's the first. It recognizes the need for a limitation on the payment of profits and allows the partners to vote at a later date to set a precise limit on payouts.

### Clause 21. Restriction on Payments—By Vote of Partners

*In determining the amount of profits available for distribution, allowance will be made for the fact that some money must remain undistributed and available as working capital, as determined by a vote of __[specify vote requirement, for example, "all partners" or "a majority of partners"]__ .*

■

Here's the alternative clause that allows you to set a specific limit in your agreement on the payment of profits to partners:

### Clause 22. Restriction on Payments—According to Preset Formula

*The aggregate amounts distributed to the partners from the partnership profits each year shall not exceed __[specify dollar limit or other formula, for example, "x percent of any net income of the above $ "]__ .*

## Draws to Partners

A draw is an advance of anticipated profits paid to a partner, or partners. Many small business partnerships handle draws informally. If all partners decide that all can take a draw, they do. If the partners divide profits equally, each takes an equal draw. If there's an unequal division of profits, there's usually an unequal draw.

The situation is different if some, but not all, partners will receive a draw. This might be appropriate if one, or some, partners actively work in the business and the others don't, especially if the working partner needs an ongoing income from the business. If only some partners will receive a draw, you need to state that in your agreement.

 No matter what the need, we believe it's usually not advisable to allow draws for some partners and not others. One reason for this is that it's hard for most new small businesses to accurately track their profits and losses on a weekly or monthly basis, so determining an appropriate figure as a draw against profits is often very difficult. If a working partner needs an income from the business, it's better to provide that by a moderate salary which, like any other business expense, can be paid whether the business is immediately profitable or not (use clause 31 for this purpose if you wish.)

We advise against specifying the amount that will be paid in draws in your agreement. You cannot be sure, now, what your profits will be, so it's premature, if not rash, to contractually bind the partnership to pay, by draw, one or more partners according to a set schedule.

If you specifically want to authorize draws for one or more (or all) of your partners, here's the optional clause you can add to your agreement to do this:

---

## Clause 23. Draws Authorized

*The following partners:*

*Names of Partners*

_____

_____

*are entitled to draws from expected partnership profits. The amount of each draw will be determined by a vote of the partners. The draws shall be paid according to the following terms:* _[insert whatever time schedule and other terms you' ve agreed upon, such as monthly draws, etc. ]._

■

You can prohibit draws instead. We think this is usually too extreme. If all partners want to take an equal draw, and the profits are there to support it, why shouldn't they? Nevertheless, there are partnerships where partners agreed only to regular—say quarterly—distribution of profits, and did not permit draws. In the interest of thoroughness, the program includes the following optional clause prohibiting draws, unless approved by unanimous consent of all partners. This clause is an alternative to clause 23 above.

## Clause 24. Draws Prohibited

*No partner shall be entitled to any draw against partnership profits, which shall be distributed only as provided in this agreement or by subsequent unanimous decision of the partners.*

■

If you do use clause 23 to provide for draws, another question arises: What happens if the amount a partner's draws in a year turns out to exceed her actual share of partnership profits? Do you think you'd simply ignore that fact, because that partner needed all that money to live? Or does it seem fair that the partner who received more in draws than her yearly share of partnership profits have this amount treated as a loan from the partnership, with an obligation to repay?

At first, converting part of what appeared when paid to be a draw against profits into a loan may seem harsh, but the alternative maybe be worse for the rest of the partners. If the partner with the excess draws can simply keep the money, you're, in effect, rewriting the basic profit distribution clause of your agreement.

If you allow draws in the first place by including clause 23 in your agreement, you may also wish to add the following optional clause to cover draws in excess of profits:

### Clause 25. Draws Exceeding Profits Become Loans

*Notwithstanding the provisions of this agreement governing drawing permitted by partners, to the extent any partner's withdrawals for draws under those provisions during any fiscal year of the partnership exceed his or her share in the partnership's profits, the excess shall be regarded as a loan from the partnership to him or her that he or she is obligated to repay within _____ days after the end of that fiscal year.*

# Meeting and Voting Clauses

You will want to pin down at least some details in your agreement as to how partners will manage the business of the partnership. This includes matters like holding formal meetings of the partners, dividing the voting power among your partners; and specifying the number of votes required to approve a formal decision of the partnership.

# Meetings of Partners

The clauses in this group cover the voting power partners can exercise at formal partnership meetings, the date of regular partnership meetings and the voting rules that will be used at these meetings.

All groups should include a clause in their agreement that specifies the voting power of the partners. The voting power of the partnership determines how management decisions are made at meetings of the partnership. Normally, each partner is given a percentage of the voting power which is the same to the partner's ownership interest in the partnership. So, if two persons contribute equally to the partnership, each will receive a 50% ownership interest and 50% of the voting power (or one vote each).

**NOTE**    Under the Uniform Partnership Act, each partner is entitled to one vote, regardless of capital contributions or percentages of ownership in the partnership (in a two-person partnership, the UPA gives each one vote or 50% of the total voting power to each partner). You can override this default rule by specifying your own voting power percentages in the partnership agreement clause shown below.

In some circumstances, you may decide to give one partner a disproportionate level of voting power.

**EXAMPLE**    If one partner puts up all the initial cash of the partnership and another contributes an equal value of future services, the cash partner may appropriately request a greater level of voting power in recognition of the added risk associated with the up-front cash contribution.

If you are considering giving a disproportionately small percentage of the voting power to one or more partners, be careful. A partner with a majority of voting power can completely run the show, unless your voting rule clause (see clauses 28 and 29 discussed below) requires more than this majority vote to make decisions. Or put more directly, the partners with the minority voting power may have no effective power in the business. If this is what you're considering, are you sure it's a partnership you want? Does this make the minority partners really akin to investors, not owner-managers? If so, would a limited partnership or a corporation better suit their interests. Even the majority partner may not benefit if minority partners feel frozen out of management. The disaffected partner can always quit the partnership business, which presumably isn't what the majority partner wants—after all, why were the minority partners included in the first place? See *The Partnership Book* by Clifford & Warner (Nolo Press) for information and instructions for forming a limited partnership (see the back of this book for order information).

Here is the clause all partnerships should include it in their agreement to specify the voting power of the partners:

## Clause 26. Voting Power of Partners

*When making management decisions for the partnership, the partners shall have the following voting power:*

*Name of Partner*                                    *Voting Power*

_____        _____

_____        _____

Initially, the program shows the same percentages in the voting power fields as you listed in clause 8 for the ownership interest percentages of each partner. This is the way most smaller partnerships will wish to divide voting power. You can change these percentages to numbers if you think numbers are clearer (in a three person partnership, you may wish to say that each partner gets "1 vote," rather than "33%" or "1/3" of the voting power) or you can supply different percentages.

■

The next question you may wish to address in your partnership agreement is the frequency of partnership meetings. In most small business partnerships, you'll be meeting each other daily, maybe hourly, so do you really need a formal meeting clause? We doubt it. But if you want to specify that you'll have regular, formal meetings at time intervals that seem sensible to you (for example, every month, every three months, etc.), there's surely no harm in doing so (and it may be valuable to periodically review the status of your business in a formal way). Here's the optional clause you can include to allow for regular and specially-called meetings of the partners.

### Clause 27. Date and Place of Meetings

*The partners shall meet on __[date, time and place of regular meetings]__.*
*Other meetings of the partners can be called by a majority of the partners.*
*For such other meetings, each partner shall receive at least five working*
*days' oral or written notice.*

# Voting Rules at Meetings

Clauses 28 and 29 below are optional and are used to specify the number of
votes necessary to approve partnership decisions at meetings. Choose one if
you wish to cover this in your agreement.

Many small partnerships require all decisions at partnership meetings to be
unanimous; that is, every partner has veto power over management decisions.
Here is the clause to use to accomplish this:

### Clause 28. Voting Rules—All Decisions Unanimous

*All partnership decisions must be made by the unanimous agreement of*
*all partners.*

■

Some small-business partnerships distinguish between major and minor decisions, allowing a single partner to make a minor decision, but requiring a
unanimous vote at a meeting for major ones. In a practical sense, you'll allow
this anyway. You're not going to require a partnership meeting and vote each
time a partner wants to buy a box of paper clips.

How you define major and minor will depend on the personalities of the
partners and type of business. Some partners do this by adopting money as a
yardstick to define the authority for each individual partner (for example, "all

decisions involving the expenditure or potential expenditure of more than $5,000 shall be discussed and voted on by all partners"), while others handle this in some other way. For example, major decision(s) could be defined as "decisions as to what jobs to bid on, the design specifications and the amount of the bid," or "decisions about the types of food to serve, particular recipes and the formula by which to price catering jobs."

## ANOTHER EXAMPLE
Here's a (slightly legalistic and very lengthy) definition one partnership uses for major decisions:

(a) Borrowing money in the partnership's name, other than in the ordinary course of the partnership's business or to finance any part of the purchase price of the partnership's properties.

(b) Transferring, settling or releasing any partnership claim, except upon payment in full.

(c) Mortgaging any partnership property, or pledging it as security for any loan.

(d) Selling or leasing any partnership property other than in the ordinary course of the partnership's business.

(e) Knowingly causing anything to be done whereby partnership property may be seized or attached or taken in execution, or its ownership or possession otherwise be endangered.

Include the following clause (instead of previous clause 28) to require the unanimous approval of all partners for major decisions.

**Remember**    If you do not include either clause 28 or 29 in your agreement, then a majority of the voting power of your partnership as determined in clause 26 is sufficient to make partnership decisions.

## Clause 29. Voting Rules—Major Decisions Unanimous

*All major decisions of the partnership business must be made by a
unanimous decision of all partners. Minor business decisions may be made
by an individual partner. Major decisions are defined as:  [write in your
definition of major decisions] .*

■

After you decide on your basic voting rule clause, you may wish to add a
separate clause containing a special rule for passing amendments to your
partnership agreement. Smaller partnerships usually require written consent
by all partners to amend the agreement. Even if your basic voting rule clause
(28 or 29 above), would require unanimous approval of amendments, it is
wise to make this clear in your agreement. Further, a less than unanimous
vote rule for amendments may make sense for a partnership with a lot of
members. For example, if your partnership has 20 partners, you may decide
to require approval of amendments by 15 partners.

When are amendments to your agreement necessary or desirable? Some types
of business growth will necessitate a change in your partnership agreement.
For example, the addition of a new partner necessarily involves a revision of
your original agreement (if only to add the name of the new partner, her contribution, share in profits and losses, voting rights, etc.). The admission of a
partner may necessitate changes in your agreement in other ways. For example, in a business we know, a former employee became a partner by purchasing a partnership capital interest. Since he had no actual cash, he paid for
this purchase by having part of his weekly salary deducted. All this was put
into the revised agreement prepared when he was admitted into the partnership.

Even if no new partners are admitted, growth of your business may require
changes in your partnership agreement. You and your partners may decide
that the expanded business should be run differently than the original one.
Or perhaps additional cash contributions will be required, and you'll decide
that they should be made in proportions different from those originally

agreed to. Any significant change in the structure or operation of your business should be reflected by a change in the partnership agreement. There is no need to become fussy over day-to-day developments and inevitable small changes. Significant changes should be relatively unusual occurrences. Just what amounts to a significant change is up to you to decide. Some changes, such as an alteration in the distribution of profits a partner receives or assets he contributes, are obviously significant. Others, such as the decision to have more formal partnership meetings or change the accounting protocol, may or may not seem significant enough to you to warrant changing your partnership agreement.

Here is the clause you can use to specify a separate voting rule for amendments to your agreement:

---

### Clause 30. Voting Rule for Amendments to Agreement

*This agreement may only be amended by the vote of:  [specify the percentage or number of partners necessary to approve an amendment to your agreement]  .*

 We believe it's unwise for small business partnerships to allow their agreements to be amended by less than a unanimous vote of the partners. Any other method could leave one or more partner powerless. The dominant partners could simply amend the original agreement out of existence. This could leave the powerless partners with no recourse except to quit the partnership. If this kind of breakup is going to occur, it's far better to have the partners face the issue directly, through buy-out or other clauses, rather than by the indirect route of amending the agreement.

# Partners' Work Provisions

Some partnerships don't bother defining work provisions assuming that people will either be reasonably compatible or they won't. Others include provisions in their partnership agreements to deal with the various working conditions, expectations and benefits that apply to one or more partners. These provisions can specify salaries, skills to be contributed or hours worked, sick leave, vacation and numerous other provisions.

If you do decide to include these provisions in your agreement, a related concern is how specific to make them. Clauses involving management and work provisions of the partners can get very detailed, down to specifying just when office meetings should be held, or what type of pens the partners will buy. Obviously, deciding how much detail to include is a subjective decision. Some partners in a restaurant might feel strongly about the type and quality of coffee to serve and want to include it under the work provisions clause of their partnership agreement, while others would find putting this level of detail in a partnership agreement laughable. Certainly, in your conversations, you should explore any area in which you uncover potential for disagreement.

Here is the clause to use if you wish to specify working provisions or conditions for one or more of your partners:

## Clause 31. Partners' Work Provisions

*The following provisions shall apply with respect to compensation, hours worked, skills to be contributed, sick leave, vacation time, and other matters regarding work performed by the partners for the partnership:  [insert work provisions here]  .*

Below are brief discussions of different types of work provisions sometimes covered in partnership agreements.

## Salaries

You can decide to pay one or more partner a salary for work actually per-formed in the business. If you decide to do so, you may wish to make the following general statement in your agreement (we advise against specifying a particular salary or pay rate):

*Partners can be paid reasonable salaries for work they perform in the partnership business.*

You can also state that no salaries are to be paid to the partners and all money will be paid to partners as profits. Since a partnership isn't taxed itself, the tax consequences are the same whether a partner receives payment as income or as profits. (See Chapter 2, Section E or *The Partnership Book* by Clifford & Warner (Nolo Press.) Here's a sample response to cover this:

*No partner will be paid any salary, except those that may in the future be decided on by unanimous written consent of all partners.*

**NOTE**   In some states, oral contracts for partners' salaries are valid. So, if no salaries are to be paid, it may be wise to state this explicitly in the work provisions clause of your agreement.

## Skills Contributed

Some partnerships may wish to specify that all, or some, of the partners will contribute specific skills, such as working as a salesman, computer programmer, bookkeeper or cook. If so, you can use the following type of statement in your work provisions clause:

*The following partners shall participate in the business by working in the manner described:  [show partners names and work to be performed by each] .*

## Hours Worked

To prevent, or at least curtail, arguments over who is goofing off, some might want to include language in the work provisions clause specifying how many hours a partner is expected to work. Again, note how continually the issue of trust reappears throughout the drafting of an agreement. If you really trust your partners, do you need to specify hours worked? Probably not, but we know of partnerships that sunk into discord when one partner suddenly wasn't around much, but still wanted his full share of the profits. If this occurs, it may help to have your expectations in writing. Here is a sample response:

> *Except for vacations, holidays and sick leave, each partner shall work _____ hours per week on partnership business.*

## Vacation

You may wish to specify the vacation time allotted each year to partners:

> *Each partner shall be entitled to _____ weeks paid [or unpaid] vacation per year.*

## Sick Leave

Do you want to insert an express provision governing what will happen if a partner becomes seriously ill? This is a subject you should discuss, of course. But how can you know now how you'd want to handle it if it occurs? There are so many variables, including the needs of the ill partner, the income of the business and the duration of the illness. If you decide you do want a provision, at least a general one stating you do or do not allow sick leave, you can include it in your working provisions clause.

## Leaves of Absence

Do you want to spell out what happens if a partner wants to take a leave of absence or sabbatical? Are they permitted at all? If so, how much time off is allowed? How far in advance must notice of a partner's desire to take a leave be given? Can leave be taken no matter what the financial condition of the business? Does the partner receive any pay, or right to profits, while on leave? Must all partners approve of the leave?

Because there are so many questions here, there's very little we can give you for final language—just a general idea of how to introduce these provisions:

> *Any partner can take a leave of absence from the partnership under the following terms and conditions:* _[state leave of absence provisions here]_ .

# Financial Clauses

How your partnership business will deal with bookkeeping, accountings, financial statements, expense accounts and other financial issues is obviously something you need to talk through, and reach agreement on. Once you do, you can include clauses that cover one or more of these areas in your agreement, as you see fit. Below are discussions of the different financial clauses available to include in your agreement. Each of these clauses is optional.

# Accountings

You may wish to specify the types of accountings (financial statements) required to be prepared for your partnership. Below we discuss the three basic accounting clauses included in the program. The first two (32 and 33) function as alternatives to each other. The third (34) stands on its own.

It's a good idea to provide for periodic accountings. This is especially true when some partners don't have easy access to, or ready understanding of, bookkeeping and financial records. Also, if you borrow money from a bank, the bank will likely require quarterly financial statements. Quarterly accountings should be adequate for many businesses, although others will want monthly statements. Check with your CPA or other small business financial expert and get her advice on this issue before including this or another accounting clause in your agreement.

## Clause 32. Periodic Accountings Required

*Accountings of  [specify what, such as "partners' capital accounts" or "profits or losses since the last accounting"]  shall be made every  [specify time period] .*

■

In a very small business partnership, you may well not want to obligate your-selves for the cost of monthly or quarterly periodic accountings, but prefer, instead, to handle this on a yearly basis when your accountant prepares profit and loss and other financial statements necessary to prepare your tax partner-ship return. Here's a simpler accounting clause you can use (instead of clause 32 above) for this purpose:

## Clause 33. Annual Financial Statements Required

*A profit or net loss statement, together with other appropriate financial statements, shall be prepared as soon as practicable after the close of each fiscal year by the accountant or other tax advisor for the partnership.*

■

In addition to your regular accounting requirement clause (clause 32 or 33), it's a good idea to give each partner the right to an accounting if she requests one. Normally, partners have this right under the Uniform Partnership Act, but it doesn't hurt to spell this out in your agreement. You can add the fol-lowing clause to your agreement if you wish to do this:

### Clause 34. Accounting Required Upon Request of Partner

*Accountings of any aspect of partnership business shall be made upon written request by any partner.*

# Expense Accounts

The following clauses allow you to deal with the issue of expense accounts for partners, either authorizing them within set limits, or prohibiting them entirely. Again, these clauses are optional. Include either of the next two clauses in your agreement if you wish to cover this subject in your agreement.

The first clause authorizes expense accounts as follows:

### Clause 35. Expense Accounts Authorized

*An expense account, not to exceed  [amount]  per month, shall be set up for each partner for his or her actual, reasonable, and necessary expenses during the course of the business. Each partner shall keep an itemized record of these expenses and be reimbursed monthly on submission of the record.*

■

The alternative clause below does not authorize expense accounts, requiring each partner to pay her own way instead:

### Clause 36. Each Partner Pays Own Expenses

*The partners individually and personally shall assume and pay:*

(a)  *All expenses for the entertainment of persons doing business with the firm.*

(b)  *Expenses associated with usual business activities.*

## Other Financial Clauses

Below we list additional financial provision clauses that you may wish to add to your agreement. If you do include any, we think clause 37 (consent required to borrow money) and 38 (signatures required on partnership checks) are the most significant.

### Clause 37. Consent Required To Borrow Money

*A partner can borrow money on behalf of the partnership in excess of*
<u>*[insert dollar limit for unapproved borrowing]*</u>  *only with prior consent of all partners.*

Be careful when borrowing money to establish or quickly expand a small business, unless the partners have lots of experience running the same type of business. Too often money borrowed to set up a business is spent on the wrong things. In our view, it's best to borrow only for absolutely essential items and, even then, to borrow as little a possible. For example, leasing used equipment will cost a fraction of purchasing it new, and gives you a chance to determine what you really need and what you can do without. If you do decide to borrow money, or provide for the possibility, it's best to require the consent of all partners for any significant borrowing as provided in the above clause.

## Clause 38. Signatures Required on Partnership Checks

*All partnership funds shall be deposited in a bank or other financial institution in the name of the partnership and shall be subject to withdrawal only on the signatures of a least* <u>*[specify number of signatures required]*</u> .

Many partnerships specify that one partner alone can write partnership checks. You can edit the above clause to set a limit on the dollar amount of checks any one partner may withdraw if you wish.

## Clause 39. Maintenance of Financial Records

*Complete financial records of the partnership business shall be kept at the partnership's principal place of business and shall be open to inspection by any of the partners or their accredited representative at any reasonable time during business hours.*

Clause 34, discussed earlier, requires the partnership to make accountings of any aspect of partnership business upon the request of a partner. Whether or not you include that clause in your agreement, you may want to include clause 39 above to at least let partners inspect partnership records at any reasonable time.

■

The next clause requires all partnership checks to be deposited in partnership accounts, not in the personal accounts of the partners. Even though this is a fundamental principle of partnership law, you may wish to include this provision in your agreement as a reminder.

### Clause 40. Deposit of Partnership Funds in Partnership Accounts

*All partnership funds shall be deposited only in bank accounts bearing the partnership name.*

■

In special cases, a partnership collects and holds money on behalf of a client. For example, when a lawyer collects a settlement check, part of it belongs to the client and must be deposited in a special clients' trust account. Money belonging to third parties should always be put in a trust, not a partnership, bank account. Of course, many businesses will never have occasion to receive money belonging to others, so they will not need to include this type of clause in their agreement. Here's the clause to use to authorize the opening of a clients' trust account.

### Clause 41. Authorization of a Client (Trust) Account

*All monies that do not belong to the partnership shall be deposited in a trust account established in the partnership's name at _____ _____ bank, and shall be kept separate and not mingled with any other funds of the partnership.*

# Outside Business Activities by Partners

A key partnership question is whether partners can engage in outside business. Often they must, at least at first, because the partnership business income is not sufficient to support the partners. If partners can engage in outside business, what types are permitted? Allowing partners to compete, even indirectly, with the partnership obviously risks serious conflicts of interest.

**Remember**    Partners are fiduciaries vis-a-vis one another. This bit of legal jargon means that they owe complete loyalty to the partnership and cannot engage in any activity that conflicts with the partnership's business without the consent of all partners.

How do you determine what, if any, competition is allowable? If the partners are running a restaurant, can a partner be an owner of a delicatessen? Work in a delicatessen? This may be an important area to cover in your agreement, because people can feel vital interests are at stake, including the integrity of the partnership and the ability to make enough money to live, or live comfortably. So take the time to talk this out and, if you choose one of the clauses below, be sure you all agree on the meaning of language used in the clauses (for example, what the phrase "materially interfere with the business of the partnership" means). Surprises and misunderstandings here can lead to much unpleasantness.

Here are the three optional clauses in the program that take three different approaches to this issue. Include one of them if you wish to cover this subject in your agreement.

## Clause 42. Outside Activities Permitted Except Direct Competition

*In addition to the business of the partnership, any partner may engage in one or more other businesses, but only to the extent that this activity does not directly and materially interfere with the business of the partnership and does not conflict with the time commitments and other obligations of that partner to the partnership under this agreement. Neither the partnership nor any other partner shall have any right to any income or profit derived by a partner from any business activity permitted under this clause.*

■

### Clause 43. Specific Outside Activities by Partners Permitted

*The following are non-competing business activities that each partner plans or may do outside the partnership business. Each partner is expressly authorized to engage in these activities if he or she so desires: [specify outside business activities that the partners can engage in] .*

### Clause 44. Outside Activities by Partners Restricted

*As long as any person is a member of the partnership, he or she shall devote his or her full work time and energies to the conduct of partnership business, and shall not be actively engaged in the conduct of any other business for compensation or a share in profits as an employee, officer, agent, proprietor, partner, or stockholder. This prohibition shall not prevent him or her from being a passive investor in any enterprise, however, if he or she is not actively engaged in its business and does not exercise control over it. Neither the partnership nor any other partner shall have any right to any income or profit derived from any such passive investment.*

# Buy-Out Clauses

This is very likely the most important subject covered by a partnership agreement, yet it's one that many people will be tempted to avoid. When you're excited and full of energy about establishing a new business, it may seem silly, even destructive, to worry about a partner taking off. What a drag. But hopefully, you know enough now about life with a capital "L" to agree with our emphatic demand that you pull back, breathe deeply and admit that negative things do happen. You owe it to yourselves to consider what you'll do if one of you—a partner—were to voluntarily leave, become disabled or die.

Sooner or later—and our experience tells us it's more likely to be sooner—
the make-up of your partnership will change. A partner may want to leave for
all sorts of reasons—to start another business, or move to Paris. Or after
many years, if you all stay together, a partner will retire or die. However a
partner leaves, the same fundamental issues come up. What happens to the
partnership? Can the departing partner sell his interest? Do the remaining
partners, or partner, have the right to buy it? How is the purchase price determined? What are the departing partner's rights and duties?

It's essential you include in your partnership agreement a clause to handle
what will happen if a partner leaves the partnership. It's patently undesirable
to leave this questions open and unresolved. If you haven't provided one or
more clauses to deal with this issue, and a partner leaves, there's a serious risk
of conflict—a departing partner's interest is often directly opposed to that of
those who remain. And if, as has been known to happen, either side or both
sides harbor grievances against the other, matters can become even more
hostile and conflicted.

In discussing this issue with your partners and incorporating buy-out  clauses
in your agreement, you'll be making rules for your joint endeavor—rules that
are legally enforceable. There's a sense of security which comes to relation-
ships when people know what to expect if things go wrong. Some people
worry that focusing on problems of a partner's leaving casts a pall over their
discussions. Well, it should cast a shadow of possible reality, but it doesn't
need to be a pall. Squarely facing the fact that problems can arise is some
assurance that they won't and a good indication that they will be dealt with
sensibly if they do.

Here are just some of the partner-departure problems that can occur. Read
them with a sense of humor as well as attention. Remember, all these things
never happen to anyone.

- What happens if a partner quits? Does the reason why he quits matter?
  Would you be willing to pay him the same amount of money as his buy-
  out price whether he becomes ill with rheumatoid arthritis or runs off to
  Hawaii?

- What happens if your partner becomes mentally ill, gets Alzheimer's or is killed?

- What happens if a partner dies and her share is inherited by her spouse, who wants to cash in as fast as possible?

- Suppose your partner gets divorced and his wife ends up with a share of the business as part of a property settlement. If they're not speaking, what do you do?

Now let's look at several examples that illustrate how these problems can arise in the context of typical partnerships.

- Joe, your partner in your Florida consulting business for five years, decides to move to Austin because his wife, who's working on her Ph.D., gets a job at the University of Texas. He wants his money out of the business. How much money is he entitled to? Does he have the legal right and expectation of getting it all now?

- Four partners run a successful Cincinnati café. Three want to expand; one decides she wants to cash in and finally become a full-time artist. Can she sell her share of the business to anyone at all? If she must sell to the remaining partners, how is a fair buy-out price determined? And what is a fair payment schedule?

- Your partner in your plumbing business, Janine, is killed in an auto accident, and her will leaves everything to her abrasive sister, Laticia. There's got to be a way to prevent Laticia from trying to fix pipes with you for the rest of your life, or from forcing a sale of the business. What are your rights to buy her out?

Do we have your attention? Good. Now, to prepare a sound partnership agreement governing partners' departures, go though this section carefully, talk, discuss, argue, speculate—do all you can to pin down now what seems fair if a partner leaves. Today, no one knows if he or she will be the person who wants to leave or the person who wants to stay, so all partners should look at the question from both positions. And be sure to take advantage of the ease with which you can use *Nolo's Partnership Maker* to create new drafts of your agreement—many partnerships change their selections for buy-out clauses until all partners are satisfied with the results.

In this section, we'll cover issues concerning the transfer or sale of a departing partner's interest in the business, including:

- the right of the remaining partners to buy that interest
- refusal by the remaining partners to buy that interest
- what happens if a partners wishes to sell to an outsider
- conflicts regarding which partner can buy out which others
- the method used to value the partnership interest of a departing partner
- requiring advance notice of withdrawal.

## Sale or Transfer of a Partner's Interest

Let's look first at the clauses that cover the basic issues that surround the sale or purchase of a departing partner's interest.

You need a basic clause in your partnership agreement that specifies what happens to the interest of a departing, disabled or deceased partner. Should this occur, the other partners normally want at least an option to buy her share and continue the business. Otherwise, if one partner withdraws, there can be unfortunate consequences, such as:

- The business may have to be liquidated. Selling off your used computers and machinery, and the sofa in the waiting room, isn't going to make much money for anybody. Most businesses are worth far more as operating entities than they are as a collection of assets up for sale to the highest bidder.

- A withdrawing partner may attempt to sell or transfer his interest to an outsider without all partners' consent. Obviously this raises the possibility of all sorts of unhappy scenarios.

- In the case of the partner withdrawing as a result of disability or death, the surviving partners may be left to deal with guardians or inheritors who will try to sell off the deceased partner's interest or actively participate in the business.

To avoid all these unpleasant possibilities, include the following clause in your agreement. It is a general clause that gives the remaining partner or partners the right to purchase the interest of any partner who leaves the partnership for any reason.

## Clause 45. Sale of Departing Partner's Interest to Remaining Partners

*Except as otherwise provided in this agreement, if any partner leaves the partnership, for whatever reason, whether he or she quits, withdraws, is expelled, retires, becomes mentally or physically incapacitated to the extent that he or she is unable to function as a partner, or dies, then the partner, or his or her estate, personal representative, trustee, inheritors or other successors in interest, shall be obligated to sell the departing partner's interest in the partnership to the remaining partner or partners. The remaining partner or partners shall be entitled to buy that interest under the valuation method and other terms and conditions set forth in this agreement.*

**NOTE**   The above clause refers "remaining *partner* or partners." This covers the situation where one person leaves a two-person partnership (the remaining partner can buy the departing partner's interest, in effect, ending the partnership and creating a sole proprietorship).

**Buying Out Inheritors, Breaking the Rules, Etc.**   What happens if someone inherits a share of the business and would prefer not to be bought out by the remaining partners? Under the above buy-out clause, the inheritor has no right to force himself into the partnership. He must sell if the partnership enforces the above clause. The remaining partners, of course, always have the right to take the inheritor (or anyone else) in as a new partner. This is an example, and a reminder, that any rules you establish in a partnership agreement can be changed later if all agree.

■

OK. The next important issue to cover in your partnership agreement is: What happens if a partner leaves and the remaining partners don't want to, or can't afford to, buy out the interest of the departing partner (as provided in the basic buy-out clause 45 covered above)?

In thinking about ways to handle this refusal-to-buy problem, first understand that an entire business is often much more salable than a share of a business. So if the remaining partners refuse to buy the interest of a departing partner, often the best solution is to sell the whole business and divide the proceeds. This gives the remaining partners a choice—buy the departing partner's share of the business or lose their own. An important decision here is how long the remaining partners have to make up their minds whether to buy the departing partner's share after she leaves. A common period is six months. That gives them a reasonable time to see how the business works without the departing partner. But you are definitely free to choose any time period you all agree on.

Here is the clause you should include in your agreement to accomplish this purpose. It is designed to be used with clause 45.

## Clause 46. Partners' Refusal or Inability To Purchase Interest

*If the remaining partner or partners do not purchase the departing partner's share of the business according to the terms provided in this agreement, within   [number of days after which the partnership will be sold]   days after the departure of the partner, the entire business of the partnership shall be put up for sale and listed with the appropriate sales agencies, agents or brokers.*

■

Now let's look at the issue of whether outside buyers should be considered as purchasers of a departing partner's interest. The previous clauses allow the partnership, and the partnership only, the right to buy out a departing partner. If it (the remaining partner or partners) can't, then the partnership must be put up for sale. Many partnerships decide to leave it this way. This means the remaining partners can never be forced into business with someone they don't like. Of course, when the time comes, the remaining partners could still voluntarily permit the departing partner to sell to an outsider if they did like this new person. There is, after all, a real incentive for this—the remaining partners won't have to pay any money (from the business or from their own personal assets) to purchase the interest of the departing partner if an outsider buys it instead.

Other partnerships decide that they do not want to compel a departing partner to take a lesser price than she'd get from a bona fide outside buyer (remember, you will adopt a separate clause that normally controls the price the partnership pays for a departing partner's interest). In these cases, they add a clause to their agreement that makes the partnership buy the interest of the departing partner for the price, and on the other terms and conditions, that any outsider offers. If the remaining partner or partners choose not to buy the interest under these "outside" terms, then the departing partner can sell to the outsider. Of course, a keyword here is "bona fide." The offer must be real, not just concocted by the departing partner to increase the price that the remaining partners will pay.

Below is the clause that provides this extra buy-out option. Because clause 45 (and buy-out valuation clauses 50 through 54) begin with the words "Except as otherwise provided in this agreement," if you adopt this clause it will take precedence over your other buy-out clauses if there is an outside buyer. If you don't want to allow a departing partner the right to offer her interest to outside buyers, but want her only to be able to sell to the current partners for a price determined under your agreement, don't include this clause in your agreement.

### Clause 47. Offer To Purchase From Outsider

*If any partner receives a bona fide offer to purchase his or her interest in the partnership, and if the partner receiving the offer is willing to accept it, he or she shall give written notice of the amount and terms of the offer, the identity of the proposed buyer, and his or her willingness to accept the offer to each of the other partners. The other partner or partners shall have the option, within  [number of days for purchase by partners ] days after the notice is given, to purchase that partner's interest on the same terms as those contained in the notice.  If the remaining partner or partners do not exercise this option and purchase the departing partner's interest, the departing partner may sell his or her interest to the proposed buyer under the terms contained in the notice.*

Including this clause in your agreement can make it fairer for a departing partner, assuming she can find a buyer who will pay a good price for her interest (a big assumption, usually). If so, she can receive that price, either from her partners (since they get first shot) or the buyer. But what if there is no outside buyer? Again, the value of the departing partner's interest in the business will then be determined by the buy-out valuation clause that you include in your agreement (see clauses 50 through 54 below).

# Conflicts Regarding Right To Buy a Departing Partner's Share

Now let's examine some possible conflicts regarding right-to-buy provisions, and look at the clauses in the program designed to cope with them. What happens if two equal partners (or an equal number of partners on both sides) can't get along, and each wants to buy the other out. How is it decided who has the right to buy? The obvious answer is that it can't be decided, unless you've added a clause to your agreement to resolve this question or, when the problem develops, you work out some sort of compromise acceptable to both. If you have no pre-arranged agreement, and neither side will compromise, under the terms of the Uniform Partnership Act, the business will have to be liquidated and the net proceeds distributed to the ex-partners. If there's a buy-out conflict in a multi-member partnership, it's possible that the majority could expel the minority (if allowed in the agreement) and then buy out their interest under the agreement. This is obviously a drastic solution, and the bitterness created will surely damage the business.

In a two-person or even-membered partnership, there's a real possibility of a deadlock. To prevent a forced sale, you can adopt any reasonable method to see who leaves and who stays. Commonly used methods include the coin flip and auction bidding procedures. Use one of the next two optional clauses below in your agreement if you wish to anticipate this potential problem.

Here's the coin-flip method clause. It may seem simplistic, but nevertheless lots of partnerships use it because it has the great virtue of simplicity: "Heads I get to buy, tails you do."

## Clause 48. Buy-Out Conflicts—Coin Flip

*If the partners cannot agree on who has the right to purchase the other partners' interest in the business, that right shall be determined by the flip of a coin as follows:  [specify, if you can, who will flip the coin and any other details important to you] .*

■

Here's the alternative auction bidding clause. With auction bidding, each side offers a price for the business, and can then bid their price up, until the highest bid wins.

## Clause 49. Buy-Out Conflicts—Auction Bidding

*If the partners cannot agree who has the right to purchase the other partners' interest in the business, that right shall be determined by an auction, where each partner or group of partners shall bid on the business, with the right to raise their bids until one partner or group of partners drops out. The partner or group of partners eventually offering the highest bid shall have the right to buy the lower bidding partner's or group of partners' shares of the business. The buying partner or group shall pay for the purchased shares of the business under the terms provided in this agreement.*

**EXAMPLE**    Bob and Skip each tire of the other and decide to end their boat/marina partnership. Bob wants very much to continue the business. He and Skip both believe the market value for their business is roughly $120,000 to $140,000. Bob offers to buy Skip's share of the business at $66,000, figuring Skip will decide to sell because Bob's price is towards the high side. But Skip counters with $69,000 for Bob's share. Now Bob has to decide whether to bid near maximum for the business or cash out. Bob's a gambler, so he bids $69,500. Skip decides that's good enough—he almost sold for $66,000. He sells his share to Bob and moves to Florida.

**Paying the Buy-Out Price in a Conflict Situation**    Providing a clause which determines who has the right to buy when partners are in conflict doesn't cover how the prevailing partner will pay the losing partner the buy-out price. To accomplish that, you need a specific payment clause in your agreement (see clause 55). You also need a clause to determine the buy-out price (see clauses 50 through 54 ) if you don't use the auction bidding clause.

## Buy-Out Valuation Clauses

A buy-out valuation clause in a partnership agreement defines the price, formula or other terms that will be used to place a value on a departing partner's interest in the partnership. Unless another clause in your agreement overrides this valuation formula in special circumstances (for example, see clause 47, Offer To Purchase From Outsider, clause 49, Buy-Out Conflicts—Auction Bidding, and clause 56, Varying the Buy-out Price), the value set here is the price the remaining partner or partners must pay to purchase the interest of a departing partner.

There is usually no outside market for the interest on a small partnership, even if it's a successful business. This fact raises a serious problem, even if the existing partners are willing to buy out the person who is leaving. Without a price determined by an open market, how do you create a fair method for determining the worth of your business? For many businesses, there is no easy solution. The best you can do is work up a method that seems tolerable, or, at least, better than other possible methods. It's akin to Winston Churchill's description of democracy as "the worst system of government ever invented, except for any other that's been tried."

So, what can you do? Below we discuss the basic buy-out valuation clauses included in the program that offer different solutions to this problem. You will want to include one of the clauses from clause 50 through 54 in your agreement.

For most beginning businesses, the market value of assets valuation method (clause 50 below) is probably the most appropriate, at least to start, since your beginning partnership is probably worth no more than the resale value of its tangible assets. In the future, you may decide to re-evaluate your situation and adopt a buy-out valuation clause that takes goodwill, earnings and other factors into account in valuing partnership interests (see clause 52). As long as all partners agree, making this change is easy. All you need do is reload your agreement into the program, remove the old valuation clause, add the new one, then print your new agreement and have all partners sign it.

## IF YOU THINK YOU NEED MORE DETAIL

Although we cover the most common types of valuation methods in the clauses below, we do not provide sophisticated valuation methods individually tailored to specific types of businesses. Occasionally, a more industry-specific approach might seem to lead to a more accurate estimation of the worth of your business. For the vast majority of small businesses, though, especially beginning ones, such detailed methods merely bog you down in complexities, without leading to fairer results.

If you decide you now want to go beyond the basic clauses we provide in the program, you can explore several routes:

- Consult with an expert, such as an experienced business appraiser or a trusted accountant who has experience with the valuation methods commonly used for your type of business.
- If you know other people in your business, you might also wish to discuss with them how they go about valuing their businesses. There are rough valuation norms based on profits, sales and cash flow for some types of businesses. But again, these usually don't help much until you have been in business for awhile and have a solid earnings history.
- Research the matter. Bookstores and libraries usually contain several books with information, advice and specific formulas that can be used to value different types of privately-held businesses.
- If you do come up with your own language for a valuation clause, you can edit the language of one of the program clauses (50 through 54) or you can include your language in clause 78. This is a blank clause set aside by the program for any custom provisions you wish to add to your agreement.

Here's a good way to think about choosing your valuation clause. It's wise to structure your agreement so that the business is given the maximum chance to survive. If the buy-out price is too high, the remaining partners may simply decide to liquidate the business. If they do, and the business can't be sold to outsiders, everyone will likely receive much less than if the existing partners bought out the departing one and the business continued. For example, if a dog-grooming business is ended, the money received from the sale of second-hand dog-grooming equipment and other business assets will probably be much less than a share in the ongoing business.

The timing of the buy-out payments (see clause 55 below) will often impact your decision on the best valuation method. Often a somewhat higher buy-out price may be acceptable to the remaining partners in exchange for reasonable monthly payments (instead of a lump sum). Also it's helpful—although often difficult with new businesses—to make some earnings projections and see how a buy-out method looks in the context of the amount of cash that's likely to be available. For example, if you're being bought out—or buying—in a couple of years, does what you would receive seem like a fair price if the partnership profits are $5,000 or $500,000? What about if the business isn't profitable but soon should be?

Finally, if you are entering a partnership where the major assets are each partner's customers, and a departing partner will likely take those customers with him if he leaves, ask yourselves what will be left that the departing partner or partners should be paid for? This is a common problem in some types of service businesses, like architects or haircutters. The answer often is that only the fixed assets need to be valued such as desks, computers and chairs.

## BUY-OUT VALUATION CLAUSES AND THE DEATH TAXES

One additional possible benefit of buy-out valuation clauses involves death taxes. If the estate of a deceased partner is worth over $600,000, it will be subject to federal estate taxes unless it's left to a surviving spouse. Also, many states impose death taxes. If a deceased partner's estate is likely to pay death taxes, the value of his partnership interest must be independently evaluated, unless there's a buy-out valuation clause in the partnership agreement. Often an independent death tax evaluation produces a higher figure for the worth of a business than the worth determined under a buy-out clause. If there is one, the IRS will normally accept what you say your deceased partner's share is worth, if the clause contains the following provisions:

- The people who inherit part of the business are obligated to sell it.
- The remaining partners are obligated to purchase the business interest of their dead partner, or they have an option to purchase it.
- The partnership agreement forbids partners from disposing of their interest during their lifetimes without first offering it to the other partners.
- The agreement is the result of an arm's length transaction, that is, it cannot be a (disguised) gift.

The asset valuation[2] method of valuing a business is based on the current net worth of the business (market value of assets minus liabilities). It is often the best clause for most beginning partnerships to use. Here's how it works. As of the date the departing partner leaves, the net dollar worth of all partnership assets is calculated and all outstanding business debts deducted to determine net worth.

The net worth of business assets is defined in this clause as the market value of the following assets:

- Tangible property, real or personal, owned by the business; this includes the present value of salable inventory, plus all other items, from manufacturing machinery to the lamps in the waiting room

---

[2]This is the method the Uniform Partnership Act requires if your partnership agreement fails to include a valuation method.

- Plus liquid assets owned by the business, including cash on hand, bank deposits and CDs or other moneys

- Plus accounts receivable

- Plus earned but unbilled fees which are likely to be collected

- Plus money presently earned for work in progress; this is particularly important in professional partnerships—an architectural firm, for instance—but it can also apply where construction work is being done, or anywhere else where money is earned although a bill had not yet been sent out. This, technically, is not an account receivable

- Minus the total amount of all debts owed by the business (net worth is assets minus liabilities.

**EXAMPLE**   *Asset Valuation Method*   Lou, Wilbur and George have been equal partners in a part-time computer repair business for four years. Lou quits. The partnership agreement includes the asset valuation method clause. The value of the assets includes all cash in the bank, fixed assets (such as tools, building, etc.), accounts receivable (money people still owe them for fixing their computers) and earned but unbilled fees, and money presently earned for work in progress. These assets are all added up and then any money the business owes (liabilities) is deducted to determine the total value of the business. Lou is entitled to a third of this net worth figure for his third interest in the partnership.

As mentioned, the asset valuation method is sensible for new businesses. Aside from your hopes, what does your business really have except its fixed assets? This method can also make sense for a business whose worth is basically determined by the value of tangible possessions, such as an antique store. However, for many businesses which have been established and profitable for awhile, this method fails to include intangible, but still real, aspects of a business' worth. Ongoing businesses are often worth more than the value of assets minus liabilities.[3]

**EXAMPLE**   *Worth of Intangible Assets*   Suppose the computer repair business we mentioned above has a net worth, under the assets valuation method, of $75,000, including: $23,000 worth of equipment, tools and office furniture; $41,000 in billed fees owed; $14,000 in earned but unbilled fees; $2,000 cash; minus $5,000 owed on the business' line of credit. But thanks to several very profitable service contracts, profits have averaged $90,000 a year for the past four years, and the partners have only worked a day or two a week. Under the asset-valuation method, Lou's interest is worth $25,000—one-third of the total value of $75,000. But the profits he's been earning are $30,000 a year.

When Lou leaves, the remaining two partners won't be able to simply divide up his yearly profits. They'll either have to work harder or hire someone to do Lou's work. Still, Lou's interest in the business seems worth substantially more than $25,000. Wouldn't you be glad to pay $25,000, and work a day or so a week, for $30,000 a year?

Some profitable ongoing businesses are worth significantly more than the value of their tangible assets because they've earned a good business reputation. That reputation brings in continued business. This intangible asset is traditionally labeled "goodwill," and is generally defined as "the well-founded expectation of continued public patronage." The concept is especially applicable for successful retail businesses (for example, a restaurant with an excellent location and good reputation), but is often less of a factor with businesses that depend primarily on individual service. A carpenter or podiatrist may have acquired personal goodwill, but it's usually hard to transfer that goodwill to another person.

Here is the asset valuation method clause contained in the program:

---

[3]But don't get too carried away with assigning big dollars to intangible assets such as goodwill. Bernard Kamoroff, author of the highly respected (by us too!) *Small-Time Operator* (Bell Springs Press), says that extra worth for many small businesses in Main Street America is a fantasy. Basically, he claims, unless thay are unusually profitable (most aren't), they either sell for the value of inventory and fixtures or at a very small premium.

## Clause 50. Market Value of Assets Valuation Method

*Except as otherwise provided in this agreement, the value of the partnership share of a departing partner shall be arrived at by determining the net worth of the partnership as of the date a partner leaves, for any reason. Net worth is defined as the market value, as of that date, of the following assets:*

1. *All tangible property, real or personal, owned by the business;*

2. *All the liquid assets owned by the business, including cash on hand, bank deposits and CDs or other moneys;*

3. *All accounts receivable;*

4. *All earned but unbilled fees;*

5. *All money presently earned for work in progress;*

*less the total amount of all debts owed by the business.*

Note that this clause (and other valuation clauses covered below) begins with "Except as otherwise provided in this agreement." The reason for this provision is that you may wish to adopt other clauses that override this valuation method in special cases (see clause 47, Offer To Purchase From Outsider, above, and clause 56, Varying the Buy-out Price in Special Circumstances, below).

## USING BOOK VALUE IN YOUR VALUATION METHOD

A variation of the assets valuation method is called the "book value" method. This means calculating the value of all partnership assets and liabilities as they're set forth in the partnership accounting books, which basically means their acquisition cost (instead of their "market value"). This method has simplicity to recommend it, but little else. The book value of items bears little relation to reality since the acquisition cost of property is unlikely to be its current worth. Some property, particularly real estate, can be worth much more than its acquisition cost. Other property, from inventory to office furniture, is probably worth less than acquisition cost. These assets may have been depreciated on the books, but even with depreciation, usually taken for tax purposes, the book figure may not be close to what the assets can be sold for. In addition, significant assets, such as earned but unbilled fees and money earned for work in progress, aren't included at all. Finally, the book value method does not cover goodwill. If, for some reason, you disagree with this analysis and wish to use book value. You can edit the asset valuation clause in the program to specify book value, not market value, as the measure of the value of your assets. Obviously, we don't think this is a sensible way to go.

## EDITING THE ASSET VALUATION CLAUSE TO ADD GOODWILL

If you feel sure that you will want to include goodwill in your business valuation, you can edit the above clause to add it to the list of assets to be valued. However, if you do, be aware that this just puts off the problem of valuing something that is, by definition, hard to value. If you decide goodwill is, or will soon be, a valuable asset of your business, you probably will wish to adopt clause 52 (Capitalization of Earnings Valuation of Partnership) as your valuation clause—it takes goodwill into account in valuing the worth of the partnership.

■

Under the set-dollar method, the partners agree in advance that if one partner departs from the partnership, the others will buy out his share on the basis of a pre-established price. Assigning a definite value to the business has the advantage of being certain, but nevertheless may not be advisable for many partnerships. Why? Because any price selected is bound to be at least somewhat arbitrary and, by the time a partner leaves, unrelated to the real current value. One way to solve this problem is to require that the partners establish a value for the partnership every year by a specified date.

The attraction of the set-dollar method with yearly updates for many partnerships is that it combines fairness and simplicity. The buy-out price is fair because all agreed to it. Once the price is determined, you don't need to bother with appraisals, accountants or earning-multiples if a partner leaves. In effect, the set-dollar method says, yes, valuation of a small business partnership that can't readily be sold on a market is inherently subjective. So we—the partners—will face that subjectivity ourselves, directly, rather than look to some other valuation method to cope with it. Since with a set-dollar method the partners must sit down regularly and work out the business' worth, this can help keep all partners up-to-date on valuation issues, and quite possibly diffuse potential disputes.

A set-dollar figure can be particularly advisable when the primary worth of the business is the energies of the partners, where there is no considerable inventory of goods and the nontangible assets of the business itself (name, goodwill, etc.) have little independent value. *This describes most partnership service businesses, particularly in their first few years.* From computer repairs to cutting hair, new service businesses generally don't have costly fixed assets. What they have is the energies and hopes of their owners. Rather than bother with trying to determine the worth of each term valued by the asset valuation method (the market value of secondhand computer repair tools, haircutting clippers, etc.), the partners simply determine what they think the business is worth and revise this figure periodically. After all, who knows their business better than they?

Another occasion to use a set-dollar buy-out clause is when the partners' concern is the preservation of the business and their relationship with each other. For example, we know of a two-man partnership that runs a trucking firm. Neither partner has immediate family to inherit his interest in the firm and both want to ensure the business survives the death of a partner. So they establish what they think a low dollar estimate for the worth of the business, to be used in the event either partner died. By setting a value in advance, the deceased partner's estate does not get involved in valuing the partnership interest. And by making this amount reasonably low, the survivor will not be unduly burdened to come up with the money.

Still another example where a yearly set-dollar method can make sense is when the partnership is involved in property investment—the partners hope the property will increase in value—although the amount, of course, can't be predicted. (If it could, we'd all get rich-.) A prime example of this is investing in real estate. Rather than bother with annual appraisals by professionals, which can be costly and time-consuming—as well as result in surprising discrepancies between one expert's appraisal price and another's[4]—the partners simply meet yearly and decide what they believe the partnership property is worth. Since real estate is bought and sold on an open market, the partners should be able to make a sensible estimation of the property's worth based on recent sales of comparable property.

Here's the set dollar valuation clause included in the program:

---

[4]The reality of real estate appraisals can be disturbing. A friend was in a three-man real estate partnership. Their agreement provided that a departing partner and the remaining partners would each hire an appraiser. If the appraisal's differed, they'd split the difference. Sounded fine and fair, until a partner died. The partnership owned a small apartment house. The partnership's appraiser valued the building at $280,000. The deceased's estate's appraiser (legally qualified) valued the property at $410,000. Our friend remains convinced his appraiser was right, but he and his partner had to pay far more than they thought was fair for the deceased partner's interest.

## Clause 51. Partners Set Dollar Value of Partnership in Advance

*Except as otherwise provided in this agreement, the value of the partnership shall be determined as follows:*

1. *Within  [insert the number of days after the fiscal year end for partnership valuation, for example, "90"]  days after the end of each fiscal year of the partnership, the partners shall determine the partnership's value by unanimous written agreement, and that value shall remain in effect from the date of that written determination until the next such written determination.*

2. *Should the partners be unable to agree on a value or otherwise fail to make any such determination, the partnership's value shall be the greater of (a) the value last established under this clause, or (b)  [if you wish, specify any alternate method for valuation here, such as "net worth of the partnership"] .*

**Modifying the Set Dollar Clause**    If partners want to be very thorough, they can edit this clause and add language that specifies a monthly rate of increase or decrease if a partner leaves in the middle of the year. Thus, if a partner leaves six months after the last yearly valuation, they have a formula for business valuation which includes anticipated monthly price fluctuations.

## Valuation of Partnership Based on Earnings

Sometimes the valuation of a business is based upon its actual earnings. This method is technically termed the "capitalization of earnings" method. Often, the best estimate of what a business is really worth (without, of course, a willing buyer or a public market) depends in large measure on its earning capacity. If the business is successful and likely to remain so even if a partner leaves, this method attempts to reflect the fact that there's a real value in the ongoing nature of the successful business. For example, take two restaurants that are each worth $100,000 according to the asset valuation method, but one has yearly profits of $80,000 and the other has yearly profits of $10,000. Clearly, the more successful restaurant is worth lots more than the other. The capitalization of earnings method is an attempt to reflect this.

The theory of the capitalization of earnings methods is simple:

- First, you determine what the business earns (usually on a yearly basis).

- Second, this earnings figure is multiplied by a "multiple," a pre-set number to give the worth of the business. Arriving at this multipler is half business sense and half magic. In an effort to value the present value of earnings, you should try and anticipate what will happen in the future.

**EXAMPLE**   *The Successful Furniture Store*   The four partners of Ace Furniture planned their business well. They obtained a low-rent 30-year lease on their store. Now, after five years in business, that store is, as they foresaw, in the center of a rapidly gentrifying city neighborhood. The partners are astute selectors of furniture their customers want. Sales are good and profits are well over $200,000 per year the past two years. One partner decides to leave. The partners have decided the value of the business is two times the average net profits for the past two years, or $213,000. The buy-out price is $416,000.

If you're just starting your partnership, or haven't been in existence very long when a partner leaves, it's premature to value your business by earnings. This is because you really want to use several years' profits—usually, a two- to five-year period is selected—as your base, not just one. Otherwise, you might end up choosing a particularly good, or bad, year. Therefore, you may want to adopt another valuation provision for your first years and then switch over to this earnings method later. However, it's not premature for you to explore the earnings method when your business is just beginning. If you plan or hope to switch to this method in a few years, all partners should comprehend what will be involved.

Suppose your business has been profitable for several years. Does the earnings valuation method necessarily make sense? Not automatically. Let's use another real world example to stress that you must first be sure the business has goodwill.

**EXAMPLE** *The Vanishing Business*  For ten years Marianne had been a successful therapist. Energetic and affluent, she'd been getting her Ph.D. in her spare time, at the same time she worked, cared for her family and carried on an active social life. The day she received her Ph.D. she decided to open a shoe store, because she was tired of other people's problems and she loved shoes. She took in a partner, Dana, who contributed work and a small amount of money. Marianne and her financially comfortable husband put up most of the money, and when the store opened, selling very high fashion and expensive shoes, it was primarily Marianne's extended network of friends and clients who came to buy them. Nine months later, Marianne realized that she had made a mistake. She hated being in a store all day and she realized the amount of money to be made per hour of work was exceedingly modest compared to therapy. She quit the partnership to return to work as a therapist. Thinking she could make a go of the business alone, Dana borrowed money from her grandmother to buy Marianne's share, based on a price that reflected the fact that the store was profitable. But with Marianne gone, Marianne's affluent friends no longer came to buy shoes. The neighborhood in which the store was located catered to middle-class customers, and couldn't support a high-priced boutique. The store failed and Dana lost her grandmother's money. The sad part of the story, of course, is that the business never really had any goodwill (Marianne did), and so Dana overpaid to buy out her partner.

Once you've determined that your business really has acquired goodwill, you then can sensibly use the earnings method to determine its value. There's no one set of criteria that exclusively determines how this method works. Rather, there are four basic areas involved. You must decide what to do in each:

1. What period of time are earnings measured (averaged) over?

2. What earnings are measured—gross income or net profits?

3. What multiplier is applied to (multiplied by) earnings to determine the capitalized earnings?

4. Are any other items, such as the value of fixed assets, also included in the valuation?

We've already touched on the time period issue. Let's look at the next three items individually.

## The Measure of Earnings

Should you determine earnings based on gross income or net profits? At first blush, it seems that net profits makes the most sense, because they show what matters for buy-out purposes. After all, a business with a substantial gross income but no net earnings isn't worth much, is it? Well, maybe it is. Many businesses that honestly report all their income still find legal, if sometimes inventive, ways to consume that income as business expenses, leaving little or no net profit. In addition, most small businesses can fairly easily inflate or deflate profits by decisions to hire, expand, buy equipment and the like.

For these reasons, some experienced partnership lawyers often use gross income as the base figure for the capitalization of earnings method. Our preference is still for using net profits, as long as they are fairly calculated.

## The Multiplier

The multiplier is the number by which the earnings, however you've defined them, are multiplied to determine the value of the business. Where does the multiplier come from? Hopefully, not out of thin air. It's not easy, though, to agree on a multiplier that will produce a fair result. No outsider can definitively say what a fair multiplier is for you. The best advice we can give you is to pick various numbers and make projections. Do any of them seem to give a fair buy-out price?

In some industries, there are somewhat established norms that help provide the multiplier. For example, certain types of businesses typically sell for five times earnings, while others often sell for ten or more. Construction companies, retail stores, and restaurants are examples of businesses where there are conventional multiple norms. You can obtain standard multipliers for these and various other industries from business evaluators or brokers who specialize in that industry.

You shouldn't accept these norms without lots of caution, however. The general economy or a particular local economy that affects the business in question can change so quickly that last year's multipliers can become irrelevant this year. For example, in 1989, the average publishing company in America sold for 23 times its earnings. By 1990, a less profitable and optimistic year, sales were being made for 11 times earnings. In addition, remember that no two businesses are the same. Two auto repair shops which earn $200,000 each may be headed in opposite directions as far as future profitability is concerned. One experienced partnership advisor we know says he believes the multiplier should never be higher than 3 times profits for a smaller business; anything more is likely to cripple the business. However, for somewhat larger businesses with a good earnings history, an unassailable market niche and a positive cash flow, it can sometimes make sense to pay as much as ten times earnings.

If you use a multiplier based on gross income rather than net profits, you will want to think in terms of a fraction (for example, in a fairly profitable business, one-third of gross income). Only the most profitable businesses which are on a fast and secure track will warrant paying the amount of your gross income or above.

## Other Factors Included in the Capitalized Buy-Out Price

Partners can decide that they want the buy-out price to be a combination of earnings and other factors, such as the current net value of fixed assets or the amount in each partner's capital account. Again, there are no iron-clad rules. We do advise again that you be careful not to create a method that makes the buy-out price so high that no one can pay it, and the business will die if a partner leaves.

Okay, if you want to use the capitalization of earnings method to determine buy-out price, here is the clause you can include in your agreement:

## Clause 52. Capitalization of Earnings Valuation of Partnership

*Except as otherwise provided in this agreement, the value of the partnership shall be determined as follows:*

1. *The average yearly earnings of the business shall be calculated for the preceding  [insert the time period for determining the partnership's annual earnings] .*

2. *"Earnings," as used in this clause, is defined as:  [specify definition, such as "net profits" or "gross income"] .*

3. *The average yearly earnings shall then be multiplied by a multiple of  [specify the multiple to be used]  to give the value of the business, except as provided for in Section 4 of this clause, below.*

4. *In computing the value of the partnership under this agreement, the following factors shall be taken into account:  [insert any additional factors for valuing the business, such as "the value of fixed assets minus liabilities"] .*

## Insurance Proceeds Valuation Method

A business can buy life or disability insurance on each partner. If you plan to do this (by adopting one of the program's insurance and estate planning clauses, 60 or 61, discussed later), you can state in your agreement that the money paid to the estate of a deceased partner, or to a disabled partner, by the insurance policy shall be the full worth of her interest in the partnership. This makes valuation very easy for disabled or deceased partners' interests —you do it when you decide what policy to buy or keep. Of course, it doesn't solve the question of valuing the interests of partners who leave the partnership for other reasons.

Here's the clause to include in your agreement if you wish to use this straightforward valuation method:

## Clause 53. Insurance Proceeds Valuation Method

*Except as otherwise provided in this agreement, if a partner becomes disabled or dies, the value of his or her interest in the partnership, including the valuation for estate purposes, shall be the proceeds paid by the disability or life insurance policy maintained by the partnership or other partners for that partner according to the other terms of this agreement.*

## Post-Departure Appraisal Method

Finally, you can postpone your decision on valuing your business and simply agree to have an independent appraiser determine the worth of the partnership at the date of a partner's departure. At first glance, this sounds great. "Hey, why struggle with valuation now? Let an expert determine the precise value later if we ever need to." Sadly, appraisals rarely work so easily or precisely. As we've said, many small businesses aren't amenable to precise valuation, no matter how expert the appraiser. So, all you're doing is passing the buck in the often unrealistic hope that an "expert" will arrive at a magic number for you. Or as one astute businessperson, describing the difficulty of valuing most small businesses, remarked "give me three appraisers and I guarantee I'll give you three quite different numbers."

There are several other reasons to be cautious about using appraisers to determine the value of your business. It can take some time to get the appraiser's report, unless you have the good fortune of finding an appraiser who is both experienced in your business and prompt. Also, the appraisal method (unlike the other valuation methods we discuss) makes it difficult to determine in advance what a partnership interest might be worth. This means partners don't have essential information when they need it, as would be the case when a partner is contemplating leaving a partnership.

Having presented the possible drawbacks to the appraisal method, let's turn to the positive side. Since, as we've stressed, no valuation method is precise or scientific, appraisal can, in some situations, be the best of your difficult choices. Some businesses do seem more suitable to valuation by appraisal than others; real estate is one example. Others are businesses that sell antiques or collectibles (for example, old baseball cards or stamps). Indeed, any business where there is a closely followed market that can be used to determine the price of inventory can sensibly use the appraisal method. Beyond this, the key to making an appraisal approach work is to agree on an appraiser all partners have confidence in. For example, if you and your partners are starting a small software business, you would want to appoint someone of unquestioned integrity and judgment who knows the software industry—and probably your segment of it—intimately.

Below is the program clause for the appraisal valuation method:

---

## Clause 54. Post-Departure Appraisal Method

*Except as otherwise provided in this agreement, the value of the partnership shall be determined by an independent appraisal conducted, if possible, by  [if you wish, specify name of the agreed-on person]  . The appraisal shall be commenced within  [number of days]  days after the partner's departure from the partnership. The partnership and the departing partner shall share the cost of the appraisal equally.*

**Modifying the Post-Departure Clause**   While it's possible to edit this clause to add language that sets out criteria for the appraiser to use or consider in making an appraisal of your business, we don't think this is wise. If the appraiser doesn't know her business, your criteria won't teach it to her. And if she does know her business, your criteria are likely to be more restrictive than helpful.

**PICKING A BUY-OUT VALUATION CLAUSE**

By now, all these different considerations and options regarding buy-outs valuations may seem overwhelming. You may well be at the stage where you're ready to ask yourself—do we really want to bother with all of this? Or should we just hire a lawyer to do it for us? Unfortunately, this is a false choice because turning the problem over to a lawyer won't solve it. Sure, a less experienced lawyer could say, "Okay, here's the method you should use" and you could uncritically say "fine." But a good lawyer won't be nearly so authoritarian. Instead, she will tell you to puzzle over the same issues and possible solutions we discuss here. and still leave the decision to you. This doesn't mean that you shouldn't consult a lawyer, only that you should, at the very least, understand that you will still need to become involved in choosing the best buy-out valuation option for your partnership.

# Clauses Related to Buy-Outs

In this section, we cover clauses related to the previous buy-out clauses. Clause 55 should be included in all partnership agreements and specifies the timing and amounts of buy-out payments to departing partners. Clause 56 is optional.

It's essential that you decide on a payment schedule in the event of a buy-out of a departing partner. If you fail to adopt a payment schedule, the Uniform Partnership Act provides, in essence, that the departing partner has the right to collect for the full value of her interest promptly. This can become a serious problem, especially in the event of a partner's death, since the deceased partner's estate and inheritors will likely insist on exercising this right. And if this happens, it can require the sale of important partnership assets, maybe even the entire business. Further, a forced sale of assets often brings in much less than a sale made at a more leisurely pace with time to find the right buyer.

**EXAMPLE**   *Immediate Payment*   Eric and Jack went into partnership to build a house they intended to rent. In the building stage, they became friends, and the house ended up being used as their single family home. Some years later, Eric dies suddenly, and leaves his share of the house to his daughter. Eric's daughter demands full payment of Eric's share immediately. Since there is no payment schedule in their agreement, and since Jack can't raise half the value of the house immediately, he has no choice but to sell the house.

We suggest that it's good business sense to adopt a payment method that puts a premium on the survival of the business. If the payment terms are so severe the business can't afford them, all involved will lose. And even if the terms wouldn't necessarily end the business, if they're too severe, the remaining owners may still decide "the hell with it," liquidate the partnership business and go on to other things. In ending a partnership—as in starting and running one—the best approach is that benefits should be shared fairly. But on the other side—and, of course, there's always another side—the partner leaving (especially his family, if there's a death) has a real interest in getting his money reasonably fast. No one wants to be hostage to someone else's business judgment for years to come. If the surviving partner makes bad choices, it could wipe out money that really should go to the departing partner. This can be a particularly intense concern if the departing partner is pulling out precisely because he doesn't trust the others. So you have to balance these competing and conflicting concerns to arrive at what you think are fair payment terms.

You can adopt any installment payment schedule that fits your needs—perhaps providing for a lump sum fairly soon after leaving, then a set amount each month, quarter or year until the whole amount is paid. It's also possible to provide for payments to increase or decrease, over a set number of years, or payments with interest added or not. Another payment method is to obtain a bank loan to pay off the departing partner. The remaining partners pay the bank in installments. This method, obviously, requires that the business be able to obtain a substantial loan, and that the remaining partners accept the added obligation of loan interest.

So, once again, there's no simple formula. You have to create a method for buy-out payments that suits your business and your temperaments. In many situations, payments are not extended over more than two to five years.[5] A common provision is to delay the first payment for some set time, such as 90 days, in order to give the remaining partners time to gather the money they need.

We want to remind you you're not required to stick with your buy-out payment clause when a partner leaves if none of you want to. Again, you're creating a floor, not a ceiling—the method you'll use if you don't all agree on another one later. For instance, suppose your buy-out payment clause calls for a five-year payment plan, with interest at 10% per year on the unpaid balance. Now suppose seven years later, when your business is prosperous, a departing partner says, "You know, I'd like to get as much cash as I can now. If you all agree, you can give me, right now, 60% of what I would have received over five years." Obviously, if this seems fair to the remaining partners, they can substitute it for the five-year payment plan.

Here's the clause all partnerships should include in their agreement to specify the amount and timing of buy-out payments to departing partners:

## Clause 55. Amount and Timing of Buy-Out Payments

*Except as otherwise provided in this agreement, whenever the partnership purchases a partner's interest, it shall pay for that interest according to the following terms:  [insert terms for payment of departing partner's interest]  .*

---

[5]This may seem to be a short period of time to raise all the money you'll need, but remember that if the business is prospering, you'll be able to borrow from a bank or, if necessary, you can find a new partner with capital to contribute.

## Varying the Buy-Out Price

You may wish to reduce the buy-out price or payments to a departing partner if she fails to give advance notice of her intention of leaving the partnership. And, of course, there are other sensible reasons for reducing payments to departing partners that you may want to consider. For example, some partnerships adopt different prices (or different methods for calculating the price) for a departing partner's interest, depending on the reason the partner leaves, or how long the partner has been with the partnership prior to her departure.

**EXAMPLE**    If a partner leaves during the initial stages of a business (let's say one or two years), you decide that she is only entitled to the balance in her capital account (this is her share of the partnership's current net worth).

**ANOTHER EXAMPLE**    In a professional partnership we know, the buy-out provision varies considerably, depending on whether the departing architect:

- Becomes disabled, retires over age sixty-five, or dies (this is the highest buy-out provision, partially because insurance can cover much of the cost).
- Quits to pursue some other nonarchitectural dream (for example, moves to Tahiti or becomes a full-time flute player).
- Quits, but remains an architect. (This results in the lowest buy-out provision, because it is assumed that some of the architect's clients would likely stick with him; if the departing partner remains active as an architect in the same county as his former partnership, the buy-out provision is even lower.)

Particularly if a partner will compete with the partnership, some partnerships decide to impose a severe sanction, making the price, say, one-half what it otherwise would be. Other partnerships are far more lenient, and many ignore this problem altogether. In short, there are no set rules we can give you regarding varying your buy-out clause. You really need to create your own solutions. Discuss this question carefully. If you want to penalize partners for leaving under certain circumstances, then include optional clause 56 shown below in your agreement, specifying the special buy-out terms you've agreed on.

**Important**    Any terms you insert in this clause will supersede the provisions contained in the buy-out valuation clause (taken from clauses 50 through 54) or your buy-out payments clause (clause 55) in your agreement.

### Clause 56. Varying the Buy-Out Price in Special Circumstances

*The provisions in this agreement for calculating the value of the partnership, or for making payments to purchase the interest of a partner, shall be varied as follows, for the following reasons:*  [insert any special terms that take precedence over your buy-out valuation or payments clauses] .

**Sample Terms**    "Unless physically prevented from giving notice, a partner shall give 30 days' written advance notice of his or her intention to leave the partnership. If he or she fails to do so, then each of the buy-out payments otherwise due the partner for the purchase of his or her interest in the partnership under the terms of this agreement shall be reduced by 15%."

## Clauses Related to Departing Partners

The clauses in this group cover issues related to partners leaving the partnership. Clause 57 should be included by partnerships with more than two partners. Clauses 58 and 59 are optional for all partnerships.

### Continuity of the Partnership

If a partnership has more than two members, the remaining partners often—indeed, usually—want to continue the business in the partnership form, uninterrupted after a partner departs. (If there is only one partner left, he may desire to continue the business, but by legal definition he won't continue it as a partnership.) To avoid this result—and to avoid a legal dissolution of the partnership—the partners must adopt a formal continuity clause.

Why worry about this? Because if the business is to continue as a partnership, a technical, formal dissolution of the old one can lead to unpleasant tax consequences. This can include the IRS regarding (old) partnership property as distributed to partners and therefore subject to tax (see the sidebar text, below). Even if the business will eventually be disbanded and sold, all interested persons (including the inheritors of a deceased partner) normally want the business to continue at least long enough so that it can be sold in an orderly fashion and not at a fire sale price.

If you are forming a multi-partner partnership (more than two partners), clause 57 below should be included in your agreement. It states that the partnership continues after the departure of a partner.

## Clause 57. Partnership Continues After Departure of Partner

*In the case of a partner's death, permanent disability, retirement, voluntary withdrawal, expulsion from the partnership or death, the partnership shall not dissolve or terminate, but its business shall continue without interruption under the terms of this agreement.*

**Other Continuity Clauses**    See clauses 11 through 13 for clauses that specify whether the partnership continues after a failure of a partner to make capital contributions to the partnership.

**TAX CONSEQUENCES WHEN A ONE-HALF INTEREST PARTNER SELLS OUT**

Under federal law,[6] a partnership is terminated for U.S. income tax purposes if:

1. No part of the business is carried on by any partner; or
2. Fifty percent or more of the business (both partnership capital and profits) is sold or transferred within 12 months.

If the partnership is considered terminated by the IRS, there can be serious adverse tax consequences for all concerned. All partnership property is considered distributed to the partners and is subject to tax, even if, in fact, the remaining partners want to continue the business. There are special rules for 50-50 partnerships that prevent the application of the standard tax rules here.[7] If any partner will own 50% or more of the partnership business, it is prudent to see a knowledgeable accountant or tax lawyer to see how you can minimize the chances that there will be a formal termination of the partnership if the 50% plus partner sells or transfers her interest.

## Noncompetition by Departing Partners

Many business partners decide they want to prohibit a departing or expelled partner from directly competing against her old firm. After all, a departing partner might move next door and take half the business with her. Contemplating the use of safeguards against future competition is not a sign of distrust, but simply a reasonable exercise of caution to prevent dire results and destructive conflicts if you do break up.

Forbidding a partner from engaging in his usual way of earning a living is obviously a drastic act. For this reason, courts often refuse to enforce noncompetition clauses they feel are overly restrictive. To be legal in most states, a noncompetition agreement must be reasonably limited in both time and geographical area, and be otherwise fair (that is, seem reasonable to a judge under the circumstances). Thus, an agreement that says a partner who voluntarily withdrew from a donut shop couldn't open up a competing business within one mile for a period of two years would probably be enforceable, but

---

[6]Internal Revenue Code Section 708(a).

[7]See Internal Revenue Code Section 736.

one that said he could not run a donut shop within 100 miles for 10 years would almost certainly be thrown out by a judge.

We're not in favor of noncompetition clauses in every case. It's supposed to be a free country, after all, and if your real estate, law or restaurant partnership doesn't work out, why shouldn't your ex-partners be free to make a living as they wish? However, in some cases noncompetition agreements may be fair. For example, if a partner is taught some unique skill upon admission to the partnership (for example, rebuilding fireplaces or retrofitting houses to withstand earthquakes) and the local area can only support one enterprise selling that skill, a noncompetition clause in a partnership agreement seems fair. Or if your business is a type where developing a good customer list is key, it makes sense to restrict a departing partner. Note that since any noncompetition clause must be reasonably limited in geographic scope to be legal, the worst that can happen when a noncompetition clause is enforced is that the departing partner must run her business in another community.

Here's the optional noncompetition clause you can include in your agreement if you wish to do so:

## Clause 58. Noncompetition for Departing Partners

*On the voluntary withdrawal, permanent disability, retirement, death or expulsion of any partner, that partner shall not carry on a business the same as or similar to the business of the partnership within  [specify the geographical area where competition is prohibited]  for a period of  [insert the period required for noncompetition by a departing partner] .*

The law regarding noncompetition clauses can vary in all 50 states. If this clause is important to you, talk it over with a lawyer of do some of your own legal research. You may find that modifying this clause makes sense.

**Other Noncompetition Clauses**    The program contains other clauses that restrict or prohibit partners from engaging in competing outside business activities while they are members of the partnership (see clauses 42 through 44, above).

■

A departing partner is legally responsible for all outstanding debts and obligations of the partnership incurred up to the date she leaves. No agreement between the partnership and the departing partner can alter her potential liability to outside creditors. However, the partnership can expressly assume the obligation to pay all debts of the firm, including any share owed by the departing partner. This type of clause won't protect a departing partner if the business goes broke, especially if the other partners are broke, too. But if the partnership, or any of the remaining partners, have assets to pay off old debts, the departing partner is protected.

If you wish to protect a departing partner from this type of liability, include the following optional clause in your agreement:

## Clause 59. Assumption of Departing Partner's Liabilities

*The continuing partnership shall pay, as they came due, all partnership debts and obligations that exist on the date a partner leaves the partnership, and shall hold the departing partner harmless from any claim arising from these debts and obligations.*

It's not unusual for the departure of one partner to coincide with the admission of a new one. An incoming partner can also assume full responsibility for the old partner's share of partnership debts. The new partner, however, is under no obligation to do so. And even if the new partner does assume responsibility for the debts and gives a written release to the old partner, this doesn't automatically leave that old partner in the clear (a creditor can still sue and recover from the ex-partner, but the ex-partner has the right to seek reimbursement from the new partner under the terms of the release). Clauses 75 through 77 below cover the issue of a new partner's liability for partnership debts.

# Insurance and Estate Planning Clauses

Just because there's a provision in a partnership agreement that states that a departing partner will be paid off on a set schedule doesn't mean the business will actually earn sufficient money to make these payments. Or maybe the business can barely make the payments, but doing so will impose a serious, even grave, drain on cash necessary for other business purposes. To protect themselves against these possibilities, many partnerships decide to purchase insurance against each partner's serious illness, incapacity or death. The insurance proceeds is then used to fund the buyout of a deceased or disabled partner. Obviously, these kinds of insurance don't help you pay off a partner who simply quits or is expelled.

For many partnerships, life insurance[8] can be a sensible way of obtaining the money needed to pay off a deceased partner's interest, especially by purchasing term insurance, the cheapest form of life insurance. If you do decide to go the life insurance route, consider solving two problems at once by providing in your partnership agreement that the amount of the life insurance pay-out is also the value of the deceased partner's interest in the business (to do this, use clause 53 as your buy-out valuation clause as discussed above). You don't have to tie them together however. You can use any of the other valuation clauses discussed above (clauses 50 through 54) and then make sure you buy enough life insurance to make any necessary payment if a partner dies.

Here are some useful points about using life insurance policies to finance a buy-out agreement:

- Partners have an "insurable interest" in the life of their partners, so they can buy policies on them directly. You can also purchase additional insurance to cover extra costs to the business, such as hiring a new employee, caused by the death of a partner.

---

[8]Ambrose Bierce defined the business of life insurance as "An ingenious modern game of chance in which the player is permitted to enjoy the comfortable conviction that he is beating the man who keeps the table."

- There are two different methods of buying life insurance policies: either the partners buy policies on each other (cross purchase) or the partnership itself buys the policies. For small partnerships, a cross-purchase plan is usually more desirable. This is because if the partnership itself pays for and owns the policies on the partners, it has been held in some circumstances that the proceeds of the policy are partnership assets and are included in the value of the partnership, thus risking artificially increasing the worth of the deceased partner's share. In a cross-purchase agreement, each partner buys policies on the life of each other partner and this problem is avoided.

## Insurance Policies

The next two optional clauses include insurance purchase provisions. Use one of them if you want to cover this in your agreement. The clause immediately below authorizes the cross-purchase by each partner of life (and/or disability) insurance on each of the other partners.

**NOTE**    Although disability insurance can also be specified in the clause below to fund the buy-out of a disabled partner, we expect most partnerships will be satisfied with life insurance buy-out protection only.

### Clause 60. Cross-Purchase of Insurance Policies by Partners

*Each partner shall purchase and maintain  [specify the type of insurance, namely "life" and/or "disability"]  insurance on the life of each other partner in the face value of  [insert the dollar amount of insurance to be cross-purchased under each policy] .*

■

In a larger partnership, a cross-purchase scheme is usually too cumbersome. If there are six partners, for example, each partner must buy five policies (one policy on each of the other partner's lives), which means a total of thirty policies for the entire partnership. To avoid this much complexity and paper-work, it's probably better to have the partnership pay for a single policy on each partner's life.

The following optional clause lets you do this (it is an alternative to clause 60 above). It also states that only the cash surrender value of the life insurance policies before the insured's death is a partnership asset, whereas the proceeds themselves are not. This avoids increasing the net worth of a deceased part-ner's estate by the full amount of death benefits paid under the life insurance policy, thereby saving estate taxes.

## Clause 61. Partnership Purchases Insurance Policies

*The life insurance policies owned by the partnership on the lives of each partner are assets of the partnership only in so far as they have cash surrender value preceding the death of a partner.*

■

If you use either of the above two clauses (60 or 61), the question arises of what happens to a life insurance policy if a partner quits or resigns? The usual solution is to allow the departing partner to purchase the policy, since the partnership no longer needs to pay for the protection offered by the policy. Here's an optional clause that you can add to your agreement that covers this:

## Clause 62. Departing Partner Takes Over Insurance Policies

*On the withdrawal or termination of any partner for any reason other than his or her [specify the event or events for which you have obtained insurance coverage, namely, "death" and/or "disability"] , any insurance policies on his or her [insert the type of policies purchased, namely, "life" and/or "disability"] for which the partnership paid the premiums shall be delivered to that partner and become his or her separate property. If the policy has a cash surrender value, that amount shall be paid to the partnership by the withdrawing partner, or offset against the partnership's obligations to the withdrawing partner.*

Here are some more facts you should know about life insurance:

- Insurance payments made by a partnership are normally not tax deductible.[9]

- If a partner can't pass a life insurance physical, you have a problem. But unless you think this is reasonably likely, there's little reason to worry about it in the original partnership agreement; solve it when (and if) it arises.

- The partners will eventually want to do some estate planning. This isn't a book about estate planning,[10] but we do want to alert you to the fact that buy-out agreements should be coordinated with each partner's individual estate plan. For example, if the proceeds of the insurance are payable to the deceased partner's estate, these proceeds are subject to probate and will increase probate fees.[11] In order to avoid probate, someone other than the

---

[9]Treasury Reg. 1.264-1; unless the policy is a condition for a bank loan with the policy assigned to the bank in case of death.

[10]See *Plan Your Estate With a Living Trust* by Clifford (Nolo Press). See the back of this book for order information.

[11]Probate is the court procedure required of most wills. In reality, it's a wasteful, time-consuming legal dance that costs the estate, and its inheritors, thousands of dollars.

estate of the deceased partner should be specified as the beneficiary of each policy. For instance, if a partner intended to leave all her property to her spouse, that spouse could be named as beneficiary of the policy. If the partner has a number of beneficiaries—say her spouse, several children and some friends—things get a little more complicated, but only a little. For example, by using a living trust,[12] the spouse would name the other spouse, children and friends as beneficiaries of the trust, to receive the gifts specified in the trust. Then the living trust is named as beneficiary of the life insurance policy.

## Control of the Business Name

In some businesses, the right to use the business name has great value—a famous rock band's name is one obvious example. At the other extreme, Joe & Al's TV Repairs is unlikely to be more valuable than Joe's TV Repairs. If your business name could matter, you should decide who owns it and gets to keep it if someone leaves the partnership. If there are several partners, the usual solution is to let the ongoing partnership (the remaining partners) retain ownership of that name. However, it may be that one partner really coined the name and wants to be entitled to use it if he leaves the partnership or the business ends.

Here's a real life example:

---

[12]A living trust is a basic probate avoidance device that's normally quite easy to prepare. Nolo Press publishes *Nolo's Living Trust*, software that accomplishes this task with versions available for PC-DOS and Macintosh computers.

**EXAMPLE**    BW opened a cleaner/laundry called BW Cleaners. When he wanted to do other things, he talked a friend, M, into going into partnership with him, with BW as the majority partner. M did, and the partnership continued still under the name BW Cleaners. The business became quite prosperous and well established. The name BW had acquired some "goodwill." Six years later, BW told M that he was going to dissolve the partnership and give the business to his son, which meant that M had to move on. M sued to keep the name BW Cleaners and won. He moved to another shop one block away from the old store and opened up BW Cleaners. BW's son had to get a new store name.

You should also decide what to do with the business name when the partnership dissolves. In this case, many partnership agreements allow a majority of the ex-partners to use the name in a new business.

Below are the four optional program clauses that deal with this issue. The first two (clauses 63 and 64) determine who controls the name when a partner leaves. Choose one or the other. Clause 65 deals with control of the name upon dissolution. Assuming it fits your needs, use it with either clause 63 or 64. The fourth clause in this category, clause 66, provides a different solution than any of the other clauses in this group. It states that one partner owns the business name of the partnership. This partner gets to use the name when she leaves or when the partnership dissolves. If you use this clause, do not use clause 63, 64 or 65.

## Clause 63. When Partner Departs—Partnership Owns Business Name

*The partnership business name of   [business name of the partnership]*
*is owned by the partnership. Should any partner cease to be a member of*
*the partnership, the partnership shall continue to retain exclusive ownership*
*and right to use the partnership business name.*

## Clause 64.  When Partner Departs—Control of Name Decided Then

*The partnership business name of  [business name of the partnership]*
*is owned by the partnership. Should any person cease to be a partner and*
*desire to use the partnership business name, and the remaining partners*
*desire to continue the partnership and continue use of the partnership*
*business name, ownership and control of the partnership business name*
*shall be decided by  [insert any method you choose, such a flipping a*
*coin, arbitration, etc.]  .*

## Clause 65.  When Partnership Dissolves—Majority Owns Name

*In the event of dissolution, the partnership business name of  [business*
*name of the partnership]  shall be owned by a majority of the former*
*partners. Any other former partner is not entitled to ownership or use of the*
*partnership business name.*

## Clause 66.  One Partner Owns Business Name
## on Departure or Dissolution

*The partnership business name of  [business name of the partnership]*
*shall be solely owned by  [name of partner]  when he or she ceases to be a*
*partner or when the partnership dissolves.*

The business name may not be the only partnership asset you want to decide
who controls if you split up. You can edit the above clauses to cover your
business telephone number, licenses, permits and similar assets if you wish.

# Dispute Resolution Clauses

If there's a serious disagreement between partners that can't be resolved by personal discussions and negotiations, it makes sense to have a method in your partnership agreement for resolving the conflict. If you don't, you'll find yourself fighting in court. In our view, this is unwise and litigation should, to the extent possible, be excluded as a possibility. Lawsuits, as you may well already know, are expensive, tedious and emotionally draining, and rarely produce results in proportion to their cost. As Judge Learned Hand put it: "As a litigant, I should dread a lawsuit beyond almost anything short of sickness and death." Ambrose Bierce aptly defined a litigant as "a person prepared to give up his skin in the hopes of retaining his bones."

The two best methods for resolving disputes outside of court are mediation and arbitration. *Partnership Maker* contains clauses to handle each of these alternative dispute mechanisms and we suggest you include both in your agreement.

Now let's examine how each process works, and how they can sensibly be implemented with the clauses included in the program.

## Mediation

Mediation is a process where an outside person—the mediator—attempts to assist two (or more) partners to solve their dispute themselves, by reaching a mutually satisfactory resolution. A mediator has no power to impose a decision. Many people feel that mediation is the best way to resolve disputes because it's non adversarial and encourages antagonists to arrive at a their own compromise solution. Mediation's strength is that neither person feels "I wuz robbed" because the partners discuss, negotiate and reach an agreement voluntarily. Mediation can be especially valuable where the people involved in a dispute will necessarily have some form of continuing relationship, as is often the case for partners or even ex-partners. This will clearly be the case if ex-partners are also relatives or members of a fairly small geographical or professional community.

### SHOULD YOUR PARTNERSHIP AGREEMENT REQUIRE COUNSELING

You can also include additional provisions in your agreement (see clause 78) requiring counseling, good faith discussions or other approaches aimed at resolving disputes. Personally, we're sympathetic to the motives partners have in including these provisions in their agreements, and are optimistic that, in some situations, they may serve to remind the partners of their commitments to one another if a dispute arises. However, we must also say that we're skeptical about the value of requiring these methods in addition to or (worse) as a substitute for a good, tight mediation and arbitration clause. Why? Because, obviously, if all partners voluntarily want to use therapeutic means to resolve a conflict, they'll go ahead and do it. But if feelings get truly ruffled and one or more partners refuses to be reasonable, you'll need more than a vague statement about good faith discussion to achieve a settlement.

The mediator's job is to assist the parties in communicating with each other, seeing the other's side and, hopefully, helping them to reach a compromise. By its very nature, mediation is an informal process, without formal rules of evidence and other court-like protocols. Normally, if one person thinks something should be discussed, it is. Once the parties arrive at their own solution through mediation, the agreement is normally put in writing, and becomes legally binding.

Mediation has become widely used throughout the business world. Many business people have seen it work, and learned that it helps to avoid the pains that an externally-imposed solution may create.

The most important decision you'll make when including a mediation clause in your partnership agreement is deciding on the mediator. You can postpone this decision until a dispute actually occurs, but we feel it's usually better to decide who you'll have as a mediator at the beginning. You can always change your mediator later on, if all agree to. But if you do fall into a dispute you can't resolve yourselves, you don't want to fight over who your mediator will be.

Be aware that being a good mediator takes skill—just being a decent, fair human being isn't always enough to qualify one for the job. If there's a person you know and trust who's served others as a mediator, he is likely to be a wise choice for you. Some lawyers who have been repelled by the hostility and craziness of the adversary court system have established legal practices devoted solely to mediating disputes and do an excellent job. Or, in some situations, you may want to designate a mediator with some technical expertise. For example, if your business involves complicated pieces of machinery, you may prefer a mediator who understands how these machines work.

If there is a dispute, the partners decide, along with the mediator, what issues need to be resolved. Together you also decide the rules of the proceeding. Generally, we don't believe it's sensible to set out details of how mediation will work. Since you ultimately will have to cooperate to resolve the dispute, the need to cooperate over procedural details can be a good place to start. But if you are comforted by pinning down some details now, you can go ahead and do it now if you wish (by editing and adding to clause 67 below).

If mediation is needed, here are some basic things you'll then need to resolve before holding the proceeding:

- When and where is the proceeding to take place?

- Will you limit or require a particular number of sessions?

- Will the parties to the dispute be allowed to submit a written statement of their position?

- Will attorneys or other representatives be allowed, or will each partner represent himself or herself?

- Will court-like cross-examination be allowed?

Here's the mediation clause contained in the program that most partnerships should include (or adapt for use, if you feel this is necessary). Note that it provides that arbitration will be used if mediation does not result in settling the dispute. This means that you should also include an arbitration clause in your agreement (see clauses 72 and 73 below).

## Clause 67. Mediation

The partners agree that except as otherwise provided in this agreement, any dispute arising out of this agreement or the partnership business shall first be resolved by mediation, if possible.

A partner who wishes to have a dispute mediated shall submit a written request for mediation to each of the other partners. Mediation shall commence within _[insert the number of days after the written request for mediation when mediation will begin, for example, 30]_ days after the date of the partner's written request for mediation.

The mediator shall be _[if you can, insert the name of the person who you would like to act as a mediator to resolve disputes]_ , if possible.

Any decision reached by mediation shall be reduced to writing, signed by all partners, and binding on them.

The costs of mediation shall be shared equally by all partners to the dispute.

The partners are aware that mediation is a voluntary process, and pledge to cooperate fully and fairly with the mediator in any attempt to reach a mutually satisfactory compromise to a dispute. If, after a good faith effort by a partner to participate in the mediation process, a partner feels the dispute cannot be resolved, he or she shall so notify the other partners, and the mediator, in writing.

If the partners fail to resolve the dispute by mediation, the dispute shall be arbitrated as may be provided in a separate arbitration clause in this agreement.

# Arbitration Clauses

We believe that it's essential to include an arbitration clause in all partnership agreements. Again, the mediation clause above assumes that you will also include an arbitration clause in your agreement in case mediation does not work. The basic rules governing the arbitration process are covered in the arbitration clause itself; if arbitration is ever called for, the arbitrator determines any other specifics of the process that all partners can't voluntarily agree on.

In an arbitration proceeding, each side presents their version of the dispute to the arbitrator. After the presentation, the arbitrator later makes a decision, normally in writing, which ends the dispute. All partners are bound by the arbitrator's decision, with very rare exceptions. If the losing partners decide to sue in court to overturn the arbitrator's decision (which seldom happens), the court will enforce that arbitrator's decision, unless the arbitrator was blatantly biased or crazy. In other words, once the arbitrator decides, that's it. The fight is settled, period.

Business and labor have used arbitration for years. They've learned arbitration usually leads to fair results, or a least results they can live with. Also, they realize that getting a dispute settled quickly, in a cost-effective manner, is often as important as who wins and who loses.

Below are the two arbitration clauses included in the program; select one as your arbitration clause. In the first, there's a single arbitrator. In the second, there are three arbitrators: each side selects one arbitrator and then those two select a third. All three hear the matter and decide it by majority vote. Our preference is to use the first clause which provides for one arbitrator. It's much simpler and cheaper. On the other hand, with three arbitrators, each side has chosen one who, presumably, is "on his side."

If you decide to select the clause using three arbitrators, you can't name the three arbitrators now, because, obviously, you can't predict which partners will be on what side.[13] However, you do need to decide now what would happen if the two arbitrators cannot agree on a third. So think of some method

---

[13]Except in a two-person partnership. Since there can only be one versus the other, each partner could, in theory, name "their" arbitrator now. But this is an odd way to begin a partnership, each thinking about who would serve on their side in the event of a dispute they can't resolve themselves.

to handle that problem—like naming someone all partners trust now to make the decision.

If you select the clause using one arbitrator, you can either name the arbitrator now, or wait. We suggest it's preferable to name one now, for the persuasive reason that you should all be able to agree on who to select. If the need for arbitration ever actually arises, that agreement is likely to be more difficult, or even impossible, to obtain.

Who do you select as your arbitrator? There's no one way to go about this that's inherently better than all others. You can name an arbitrator who's a trusted friend.[14] Or, you may know someone who, although not a close friend, seems fair and capable of judiciously deciding matters (and of course, is willing to take on the job). Another possibility is someone who has served as an arbitrator before. Many lawyers frequently serve as arbitrators, as do other professional dispute resolvers. Also, in many areas of the country, retired judges (colloquially called "rent-a-judges") serve as arbitrators.

One caveat about professional arbitrators: some, such as those from the American Arbitration Association,[15] are quite expensive. Check fees before you agree on any expert. If you add specific rules for the arbitration proceeding to your arbitration clause, be sure the arbitrator or arbitration organization you choose will accept your rules. For example, the American Arbitration Association requires the use of their own detailed rules.

If you have named a person to mediate disputes in your mediation clause (clause 67 above), you can also name this person as your arbitrator. That's very much up to you. However, some people decide that giving the mediator the power to impose an arbitration decision (in case mediation fails) is a bad idea since it may influence the way all parties conduct the mediation (instead of trying to agree, they try to impress the mediator/arbitrator). On the other

---

[14]Selecting a friend can result in some problems, however, if the friend later rules against you.

[15]The American Arbitration Association in an nationwide institution which provides arbitrators, who are often lawyers. In the past, they have specialized in big-time disputes and charged hefty fees. Currently, they claim to have more cost-effective arbitration programs for smaller disputes.

hand, the advantage of having the same person for both (if you adopt the one arbitrator clause) is that you don't run the risk of having to present the case twice—first to the mediator, then, if mediation fails, to the arbitrator.

Just because you name an arbitrator now does not, of course, mean you'll ever have to use her. After all, most partnerships don't fall so far apart that they can't resolve problems by themselves, or through mediation. Nor does it mean you must use that particular arbitrator, if you later decide on someone else. Years from now, if a dispute you can't resolve yourselves arises, you may all agree that another arbitrator is preferable. But if you're so far apart you can't then agree on who is the best person to decide the conflict—and this has certainly been known to occur—at least you've got a fallback position, an arbitrator already named.

OK. Here are the two arbitration clauses contained in the program. Remember, if you have included the mediation clause in your agreement (clause 67), you must include one of the following arbitration clauses as well.

## Clause 68. Arbitration With One Arbitrator

*The partners agree that, except as otherwise provided in this agreement, any dispute arising out of this agreement, or the partnership business, shall be arbitrated under the terms of this clause.*

*The arbitration shall be carried out by a single arbitrator who shall be  [if you can, insert the name of the person who you select as your arbitrator; if you can't, you can complete this phrase with the words "agreed upon by the parties to the dispute"] . If this person is unwilling or unable to act as arbitrator, then the following alternate arbitrator, or procedure to select an alternate arbitrator, shall be used:  [specify an alternate arbitrator or procedure to select an alternate arbitrator if your first choice for arbit-rator is unavailable or if you cannot agree on an arbitrator later]* .        16

*Any arbitration shall be held as follows:*

1. *The partner(s) initiating the arbitration procedure shall inform the other partner(s) in writing of the nature of the dispute at the same time that he or she notifies the arbitrator.*

2. *Within   [insert the number of days for responding to the arbitration notice]  days from receipt of this notice, the other partners shall reply in writing, stating their views of the nature of the dispute.*

3. *The arbitrator shall hold a hearing on the dispute within seven days after the reply of the other partner(s). Each partner shall be entitled to present whatever oral or written statements he or she wishes and may present witnesses at the hearing.*

4. *The arbitrator shall make his or her decision in writing.*

5. *If the partner(s) to whom the demand for arbitration is directed fails to respond within the proper time limit, the partner(s) initiating the arbitration must give the other an additional five days' written notice of "intention to proceed to arbitration." If there is still no response, the partner(s) initiating the arbitration may proceed with the arbitration before the arbitrator, and his or her award shall be binding.*

6. *The cost of arbitration shall be borne by the partners as the arbitrator directs.*

---

[16]If you can't agree upon an arbitrator later and you don't specify an alternate procedure here to pick an arbitrator (such as a coin flip to have one faction choose an arbitrator), you'll probably wind up in court.

7. The arbitration award shall be conclusive and binding on the partners
   and shall be set forth in such a way that a formal judgment can be
   entered in the court having jurisdiction over the dispute if either party so
   desires.

■

Here's the second choice for an arbitration clause where each side names
"their" arbitrator, and those two name a third:

## Clause 69. Arbitration With Three Arbitrators

The partners agree that, except as otherwise provided in this agreement, any
dispute arising out of this agreement or the partnership business shall be
arbitrated under the terms of this clause. The arbitration shall be carried
out by three arbitrators. Each partner or side to the dispute shall appoint
one arbitrator. The two designated arbitrators shall appoint the third
arbitrator.

The arbitration shall be carried out as follows:

1. The partner(s) initiating the arbitration procedure shall inform the
   other partner(s) in writing of the nature of the dispute at the same time
   that they designate one arbitrator.

2. Within _[insert the number of days for responding to the arbitration
   notice]_ days from receipt of this notice, the other partners shall reply in
   writing naming the second arbitrator, and stating their view of the
   nature of the dispute.

3. *The two designated arbitrators shall name a third arbitrator within ten days from the date the second arbitrator is named. If they cannot agree, the following procedure shall be used to name the third arbitrator:*  _[specify a procedure to be used to name a third arbitrator in case of deadlock]_ .

4. *An arbitration meeting shall be held within*  _[insert the number of days within which an arbitration meeting must be held]_  *days after the third arbitrator is named.*

5. *Each partner shall be entitled to present whatever oral or written statements he or she wishes and may present witnesses at the arbitration meeting.*

6. *The arbitrators shall make their decision in writing.*

7. *If the partner(s) to whom the demand for arbitration is directed fails to respond within the proper time limit, the partner(s) initiating the arbitration must give the other an additional five days' written notice of "intention to proceed to arbitration." If there is still no response, the partner(s) initiating the arbitration may proceed with the arbitration before the arbitrators, and their award shall be binding.*

8. *The cost of arbitration shall be borne by the partners as the arbitrators shall direct.*

9. *The arbitration award shall be conclusive and binding on the partners and shall be set forth in such a way that a formal judgment can be entered in the court having jurisdiction over the dispute if either party so desires.*

**Modifying Your Arbitration Clause**   We believe it's preferable not to be more specific about the arbitration process itself in your arbitration clause. Leave that up to the arbitrator and yourselves, if the need ever arises. But if you want more specifics now, you can edit either arbitration clause, and specify more details of the arbitration process, including:

- Can the arbitrator(s) order you to produce evidence? (Normally they have this power.)
- Must the decision be explained (that is, how and why the arbitrators reached it)?
- Is there a time limit within which the decision must be rendered?
- Will you be allowed to submit a written statement?
- Is cross-examination allowed?
- Will lawyers be allowed?

# Expulsion of Partner Clauses

Expelling a partner is a drastic decision, one you surely hope you never have to consider, let alone implement. It's often a subject that new partners find very difficult to consider, since they feel optimistic about their new enterprise and each other. However, part of our job is to make sure you considered the worst as well as the best possibilities. Also, if your business expands, you may take in new partners who you don't know as well, and it may be prudent to have an expulsion clause just in case they don't work out.

It's quite unusual for a small business partnership to expel a partner. We know of many partnerships that have dissolved completely, and some in which, say, two partners remain and one leaves, but personally we can't ever recall hearing of a formal expulsion of a partner. Perhaps this is because many partners in small businesses decide not to cover possible expulsion in their partnership agreement. They reason that since everything they decide and do must be unanimous, if they ever reach the stage where they're considering an expulsion, it's time to disband the partnership. For larger partnerships, the reality is different. Here it's usually not practical to end the business because one partner is impossible to deal with. Even though they may be used infrequently, large partnerships should decide to include an expulsion clause in their agreement.

Clauses regarding expulsion of a partner are strictly construed by the courts. For example, courts are reluctant to expel a partner, or enter a decree of dissolution of a partnership, based on the mental or bodily health of that partner. If it's important to you that all partners be healthy, or not be illegal drug users, or nonsmokers, for that matter, and you want them out if they're not, say so clearly and set up some sort of criteria by which a determination can be made. This same sort of definiteness should be the hallmark of any expulsion clause. Can a simple majority expel a partner? Do there have to be grounds justifying the expulsion? Or do you want a clause that simply says a partner may be expelled for reasons that appear to be sufficient to the other partners?

The following optional clause can be used to specify the procedure and grounds for expelling a partner from your partnership. It provides that an expelled partner receives the same payment for her interest as a partner who leaves for any other reason. By doing this, you treat the partner who is expelled the same way you treat a partner who leaves for a neutral reason and probably lower the level of bitterness that is likely to surround an expulsion.

## Clause 70. Procedure and Grounds for Expulsion

*A partner may be expelled from the partnership as follows:  [insert voting requirements and any grounds necessary for a partner's expulsion]  .*

*Expulsion shall become effective when written notice of expulsion is received by the expelled partner. When the expulsion becomes effective, the expelled partner's right to participate in the partnership's profits and his or her other rights, powers and authority as a partner of the partnership shall terminate. An expelled partner shall be entitled to receive the value of his or her interest in the partnership according to the provisions of this agreement.*

Under the Uniform Partnership Act, a partner's personal bankruptcy, technically called "becoming subject to an order of relief" from the bankruptcy court, causes dissolution of a partnership, even if the business itself is still viable. In any partnership, and especially a large one, it can be appropriate to have a provision planning for immediate expulsion of a bankrupt partner.

The following clause contains the technical language defining acts constituting bankruptcy,[17] and authorizes expulsion for a partner's bankruptcy. It is optional and can be used alone or in conjunction with previous expulsion clause 70:

## Clause 71. Expulsion of a Partner for Bankruptcy

*Notwithstanding any other provision of this agreement, a partner shall cease to be a partner and shall have no interest in common with the remaining partners or in partnership property when the partner does any of the following:*

1.  *Seeks protection of the U.S. Bankruptcy Court under Chapter 7, Chapter 11 or other provisions of the federal Bankruptcy Code.*

2.  *Obtains or becomes subject to an order or decree of insolvency under state law.*

3.  *Makes an assignment for the benefit of creditors.*

4.  *Consents to or accepts the appointment of a receiver or trustee to any substantial part of his or her assets that is not vacated within  [insert the number of days after which a partner will be expelled]  days.*

5.  *Consents to or accepts an attachment or execution of any substantial part of his or her assets that's not released within  [insert the number of days after which a partner will be expelled]  days.*

---

[17]Bankruptcy has its own rules, concepts and language. Few of you are likely to need to know about all this. If you do, rather than try and explain here what all this technical language means, we recommend *How to File for Bankruptcy* by Elias, Renauer & Leonard (Nolo Press).

*From the date of any of the preceding events, the partner shall be considered as a seller to the partnership of his or her interest in the partnership and shall be entitled to receive the value of his or her interest in the partnership according to the provisions of this agreement. If a partner is expelled under the terms of this clause, the partnership shall not be dissolved, but shall continue to function without interruption.*

# Admission of New Partners

Now let's look on the clauses that handle the admission of a new partner or partners to your partnership. This is a vital issue and should be covered in your agreement. Growth of a partnership business may lead to the opportunity, or even the necessity, of taking in a new partner or partners for any of a number of reasons. To name a few of the more common ones:

- desire (or need) for the new partner's contribution of cash
- need for skills contributed by the new partner
- need for additional management
- need to retain a key employee by allowing her to become a partner
- desire to expand your business to new locations or customers offered by the new partner.

## Vote Requirement for Admitting New Partners

The first question is the vote requirement necessary to admit a new partner. We believe that in small partnerships particularly, it's wise to require unanimous consent. The following clause requires unanimous approval for the admission of new partners.

## Clause 72. Admission of New Partners—By Unanimous Consent

*A new partner or partners may be added to this partnership only by the unanimous written agreement of all existing partners.*

### HOW TO ADMIT A NEW PARTNER

After obtaining the votes necessary to admit a new partner, make sure to prepare a new partnership agreement. With the Partnership program, amending your agreement to add a new partner is easy:

- Run the program and load the latest version of your agreement into the program (select the Document menu then choose the Load command by pressing the </>,<D> and <L> keys)
- Add your new partner's name to the list of partners in clause 1. To do this highlight one of the existing fields in this list, then choose the Field menu and select the Add command.
- Update clause 8 (contributions and ownership percentages), clause 19 (profits and losses), clause 26 (voting power) and any other clauses that may affect your new partner (for example, clause 31 that specifies the working conditions for your partners).
- Add a new clause, if you wish, specifying the liability of your new partner for partnership debts (see clauses 75 through 77 below).
- Save your new agreement and print a copy to be signed by all partners, including your new partner.

■

If a large partnership requires unanimity to admit a new partner, there can be serious problems if one or more partners refuse to accept the majority decision. One way to handle this is to require a less-than-unanimous vote for admitting new partners. Use the following clause (instead of previous clause 72) if you wish to do this:

## Clause 73. Admission of New Partners—By Less Than All Partners

*A new partner may be admitted to the partnership with the written
approval of: [specify the percentage or number of votes required for
admitting a new partner] .*

**OTHER WAYS TO DEAL WITH NEW PARTNERS IN LARGER PARTNERSHIPS**
Some larger partnerships we know (mostly bigger cooperatives) still require
that all concur to admission of a new partner, and avoid conflicts over this by
other means. First, in reality, such conflicts rarely occur. Second, there are
ways to test a potential partner to see if she'll fit in. For example, one food sales
collective we know of invites prospective partners to work for the enterprise for
several weeks. After that time, a vote is taken to determine whether the new-
comer will be accepted into the business. If it's unanimous, the hours they've
worked are credited toward their buy-in amount. However, if they're rejected
after the other partners get to know them, they're paid for their work at the
going rate (agreed upon before they start).

Further, if one or a few partners of a large partnership attempts to regularly
thwart the will of the majority regarding the admission of new partners, peer
pressure can often curtail this obstructionism. If peer pressure fails, large partnerships almost invariably have expulsion provisions in their agreement, so a
partner who consistently or arbitrarily stands alone, preventing new partners
from being admitted, may find himself rejected.

## Avoiding a Technical Dissolution When Admitting New Partners

Adding a new partner causes a technical "dissolution" of the original partnership. A dissolution of a partnership need not imply the sort of negative consequences that we associate with the term dissolution of marriage (that is, termination of the relationship). A partnership "dissolution" is simply the legal term used for certain changes in the business structure, including whenever a change occurs in the membership of the partnership. Even if the business otherwise continues as usual, there has been a technical dissolution of the old partnership and the simultaneous continuation of that business by the newly created partnership. In other situations, however, the dissolution of a partnership may signal a much more fundamental change—up to and including the partnership's ceasing to do business.

Legally, from the moment of dissolution of a partnership business, no new partnership business can be undertaken by the old partnership. The original partners only have legal authority to wind up the business as rapidly as is feasible.[18] But since, in the case of the addition of a new partner, the "dissolution" of the old partnership is basically a technical matter, the major problem is to close out an old set of books and start another. The business itself can go happily on. To make this clear, include the following optional clause in your agreement (this optional clause is not legally necessary—it serves as a reminder to your partners):

### Clause 74. No Dissolution When New Partner Admitted

*Admission of a new partner or partners shall not cause dissolution of the partnership business.*

---

[18]UPA Sections 30, 33, 35, 37.

## Incoming Partner's Liability for Partnership Debts

When you prepare your revised partnership agreement for your new partner (and all existing partners) to sign, you may wish to include a new clause that specifies the extent of the new partner's liability for partnership debts. Under the Uniform Partnership Act,[19] a new partner is personally liable for partnership debts incurred before he became a partner, up to his share (that is, contribution to) of partnership property.[20] Your agreement can repeat this default rule under the UPA or it can contain a different rule defining the liability of your new partner for partnership debts.

**EXAMPLE**   *Partnership Debt*   Raul contributes $50,000 when he joins Elaine and Beverly in a partnership to produce pet food. When Raul joins the partnership, the two women owe $100,000. Unless a specific provision on liability appears in the agreement, Raul's maximum liability under the UPA for the pre-existing debts would be the $50,000 he contributes.

The new agreement prepared by Beverly and Elaine (and signed by all three partners) could contain a clause that changes the default rule under the UPA and releases Raul from any liability for partnership debts which existed before he became a partner. Even so, the $50,000 he put up would be part of the business, and creditors could go after it if the business had no other assets. Or, at the other extreme, it could state that Raul assumes full personal liability for all existing debts.

 Regardless of the legal rule included in the new agreement, it is risky for a new partner to join a partnership with substantial debts. Creditors tend to sue anyone who's an owner of an insolvent business, no matter when the owner came on board. Whether you're a new incoming partner, or a member of the original partnership, you certainly hope that existing debts will be an academic problem and that your business is sufficiently profitable to pay debts from operating revenues. But, of course, this isn't always true. Indeed, one

---

[19]UPA Section 17.

[20]Of course, once someone becomes a partner, he or she has unlimited personal liability for partnership debts incurred after his or her admission to the partnership.

reason to bring in a new partner is precisely because the old partners need more cash.

Below are the three optional clauses for handling the issue of partnership debts and the incoming partner. They specify the name of your new partner and the extent of the new partner's liability. Choose one if you wish to cover this area in your new agreement.

Clause 75 states the Uniform Partnership Act rule that new partners are liable for pre-existing partnership debts up to the amount of their capital contribution:

## Clause 75.  New Partner Liable for Existing Debts Up to Capital Contribution

*The undersigned partner, [name of new partner] , expressly assumes personal liability for debts of the partnership incurred on or before [date of admission of the new partner to the partnership] equal to the amount of his or her contribution to the partnership, totaling [insert the new partner's total capital contribution to the partnership] .*

■

Clause 76 releases new partners from liability for pre-existing partnership debts. Many new partners will sensibly insist on the adoption of this clause prior to signing the partnership agreement.

## Clause 76.  New Partner Liable for New Debts Only

*The undersigned partner, [name of new partner ] shall not be personally responsible for, or assume any liability for, any debts of the partnership incurred before [date of admission of the new partner to the partnership] .*

■

If you want to make new partners liable for all partnership debts, then include clause 77 instead. Of course, a new partner may insist on changing this clause before signing your partnership agreement:

## Clause 77. New Partner Liable for All Debts

*The undersigned partner,   [name of new partner ]  , hereby expressly assumes full personal liability for the past, present and future debts of the partnership.*

### INCOME TAX LIABILITY OF INCOMING SERVICE PARTNERS
If a new partner receives a capital (that is, equity) interest in a partnership in exchange for services rendered or to be rendered to the partnership she will be taxed immediately for the fair market value of the interest received.[21] This can be a real problem for newly admitted partners to professional partnerships, because the new partner probably will receive an interest in the (taxable) assets of the partnership, including accounts receivable and earned (but unbilled) fees.

---

[21]The interest received must be without substantial risk of forfeiture for this tax rule to apply. Cases where there is a substantial risk of forfeiture are somewhat rare—they include instances where the partnership property has already been liened by a creditor.

**EXAMPLE**   *Tax Liability*   Philip and Betty operate a successful accounting firm. They decide to invite Janice, who has worked for them for years, to join their partnership because she's a good worker and a good friend, but also because they fear that if they don't give her a better deal, she'll open her own competing business. Janice receives 25 percent interest in the partnership and is not required to pay anything for it. The partners calculate the fair market value of this interest to be worth $50,000. Although Janice doesn't receive $50,000 cash—just her ownership interest in the business assets (that is, fixed assets, accounts receivable, unbilled fees and good will)—the IRS takes the position that she's received ordinary income amounting to $50,000, which is subject to income tax. In sum, come tax payment time, Janice will be out-of-pocket a substantial amount because she received her partnership ownership interest.

Because of this harsh tax rule (and often because it makes practical sense as well), it can be wiser for a service partner to sign a contract with the partnership that she'll receive her ownership (equity) interest in the business over time, after her services are performed. Or perhaps the partnership will agree to pay the taxes. Consult a tax accountant for assistance if you face this situation.

**LIABILITY OF DEPARTING PARTNERS FOR PARTNERSHIP DEBTS**
Departing partners remain personally liable to the business' creditors for all debts of the partnership incurred up to the time they leave. Even if an incoming partner specifically assumes full responsibility for old partnership debts, this doesn't release the departing partner from potential liability to existing creditors. Also, even a written release and assumption of liability by the new partner for the old partner doesn't automatically leave the old partner in the clear. If all the partners (including the new one) are broke, creditors of the old partnership can still go after the departed partner.

**EXAMPLE**    Al and James are partners in A-J Auto Body Repair. Al leaves, selling his partnership interest to Peter, who assumes personal liability for all existing debts of A-J. On the date Al leaves, A-J owes $36,000 to Nifty Paints, a major paint supplier. The bill is never paid, and six months later A-J goes broke. Neither James nor Peter has any personal assets. Al can be held liable by Nifty for the full $36,000 owed. Of course, Al has a claim for this amount against Peter (who assumed that debt); but if Peter is broke, it doesn't seem likely he will collect on it.

# Additional Provisions

The clause below is optional and allows you to add your own provisions to your agreement. Use it to cover as many additional areas in your agreement as you feel necessary.

 Be careful when drafting the wording of additional provisions. Your language should be clear and consistent with the other provisions in your agreement. If you have doubts, check your proposed language with a lawyer.

### Clause 78. Additional Provisions

*Insert any additional partnership agreement clause in this space:*  _[insert your provisions here]_ .

# Standard Clauses

The first five clauses (79-83) in this category contain standard legal provisions that you should include in your agreement. The final clause, clause 84, should be included if any partner has a spouse. This clause contains language indicating the consent of the spouse(s) of the partners to all of the terms of the agreement, including the partnership valuation clause. Including this clause in your agreement can help avoid additional problems if a partner and her spouse seek a divorce (as discussed below).

■

The first standard clause specifies the state whose laws will govern your partnership. Although the Uniform Partnership Act has been adopted in all states except Louisiana, you will normally insert the state where the partners live and will do business. If you plan to operate in more than one state, or the partners live in more than one state, you should normally select the state where you have your principal place of business.

**NOTE**    Because the provisions of each state's UPA differ slightly, we list the legal citation to each state's UPA—where you can find this law in your state's lawbooks—in Appendix C.

## Clause 79. State Law

*The partners have formed this general partnership under the laws of the State of  [insert the state whose laws will govern your partnership] , intending to be legally bound thereby.*

■

Here is the next standard clause specifying that any attachment pages referred to in the partnership agreement are treated as part of your partnership agreement.

## Clause 80. Attachments to Agreement

*Any sheet or document referred to in and attached to, or included with, this partnership agreement shall be regarded as fully contained in this partnership agreement.*

■

The next standard clause states that your written agreement contains the entire understanding of the partners regarding their rights and duties in the partnership, and no modification is valid unless it is done as a proper amendment to this agreement. If one partner subsequently tries to claim that an oral agreement between you has altered the written terms of this agreement, it will prove handy to have this clause in your agreement.

## Clause 81. Agreement Is Entire Understanding of Partners

*This agreement contains the entire understanding of the partners regarding their rights and duties in the partnership. This agreement may not be orally modified under any circumstances. Further, a written modification shall only be effective if properly approved and signed by the partners as an amendment to this agreement under the terms of this agreement.*

■

The standard clause below states that unless the agreement provides otherwise, the provisions of the agreement apply to those who may purchase, inherit or represent a partner's interest in the partnership.

## Clause 82. Agreement Is Binding on Successors

*This agreement shall be binding on and for the benefit of the successors, inheritors, assigns and personal representatives of the partners, except to the extent of any contrary provision in the agreement.*

■

On rare occasions, courts strike down, or refuse to enforce, a disputed provision of a partnership agreement—the clause may be in conflict with the state's current partnership statutes, may violate public policy or result in unfairness to one or more of the parties. To take one example, overly restrictive noncompetition clauses are occasionally invalidated by the courts. The next standard clause makes it clear that each provision in the agreement is separate and shall not be affected if another provision is ruled unenforceable or invalid by a court.

## Clause 83. Agreement Stands if Clause Is Invalidated

*If any term, provision, or condition of this agreement is held by a court of competent jurisdiction to be invalid, void or unenforceable, the rest of the agreement shall remain in full force and effect and shall in no way be affected, impaired or invalidated.*

■

A spouse may have a legal interest in a partnership entered into by the other spouse. This is generally true in community property states (Arizona, California, Idaho, Nevada, New Mexico, Texas, Washington and Wisconsin) where each spouse owns one-half of all community property, and may well be true in the other "common law" states as well, especially at divorce.

If both spouses have legal interests in a partnership and there is a divorce, the partnership may well have to be appraised or evaluated for divorce settlement purposes. Many partnerships understandably don't want the valuation clause included in their agreement (see clauses 50 through 54 above) ignored in a divorce proceeding. The best way to try to prevent this is to have all spouses sign the partnership agreement, too. This means that under normal circumstances, a divorce court will accept the partnership agreement valuation method as long as it's reasonably fair.

 If you are concerned with this issue, check with a lawyer to make sure the valuation and spousal consent clauses in your agreement will meet your particular needs in the event of a partner's divorce.

The final standard clause below is optional. If you include it in your agreement, it will be printed together with space for the signatures of the spouses of your partners at the very end of end of your agreement, after the signature lines for your partners (regardless of its actual position in the document panel for your agreement at the bottom of the screen).

## Clause 84. Spousal Consent

*The following spouse(s) of the partners has (have) read and understand this partnership agreement and consent(s) to all clauses and terms in it. The spouse(s) also specifically agree(s) that the business valuation method contained in the agreement shall be used in any legal proceeding to determine the value of any interest the spouse(s) may have in the business.*

---

*Signature(s) of Spouse(s)*

# Final Instructions for Preparing Your Agreement

- Select the document panel at the bottom of the screen (it lists the clauses included in your agreement) by pressing the <F3> function key. Then save your agreement by selecting the Save command from the Document menu (press the </>, <D>, and <S> keys). Replace the name UNTITLED.DOC with a more descriptive name for your saved agreement.

**Remember**   A valid DOS filename must have no more than 8 characters, followed by a 3-character filename extension. All partnership agreements must be saved with a .DOC filename extension. If you don't provide the filename extension, the program will supply it for you.

Examples of valid filenames:

AGREE.DOC, PARTNER.DOC, BEN&JERI.DOC.

- Print your agreement by choosing the Print command from the Document menu (press the </>, <D> ,<P> keys, then press the <P> key again). Your partnership agreement will be printed with signature and date lines for each of your partners.

**NOTE**  You can print your agreement to a text file on the disk by selecting the Disk command from the Print menu.

- Each partner should sign and date the printed agreement. If you have included the optional spousal consent clause (clause 84), the spouses of the partners also should sign and date the agreement on the separate lines printed at the very end of the agreement (after the spousal consent clause).

**NOTE**  A partnership agreement does not have to be notarized unless it entails the ownership of real property and you want to record it at your county recorder's office.

- Give each partner a copy of the agreement. Keep one copy at the principal office of the partnership.

# APPENDIX

# A. List of *Partnership Maker* Clauses

## Name Clauses

### Clause 1. Names of Partners and Effective Date

*This partnership agreement is entered into and effective as of*

_____, *by:*

*Names of Partners*

_____

_____

### Clause 2. Name of the Partnership

*The name of the partnership is*

_____

### Clause 3. Name of the Business

*The name of the partnership business is*

_____

# Term of the Partnership

### Clause 4. Term—Until Dissolution of Partnership

*The partnership shall last until it is dissolved by all the partners or according to the terms of this agreement.*

### Clause 5. Term—Until Specific Date or Event

*The partnership shall commence as of the date of this agreement and shall continue until _____, at which time it shall be dissolved and its affairs wound up.*

# Purposes and Goals of the Partnership

### Clause 6. Purposes of the Partnership

*The purposes of the partnership are:*

_____.

### Clause 7. Goals of the Partnership

*The goals and dreams of each partner are set out below. The partners understand that this statement is not legally binding, but include it in the partnership agreement as a record of their hopes and intentions:*

_____.

# Contribution Clauses

### Clause 8. Contributions

*The following persons shall make the following contributions of cash property or services to the partnership in return for the following ownership shares in the partnership:*

| Name of Partner | Description of Contribution | Percentage |
|---|---|---|
| _____ | _____ | _____ |
| _____ | _____ | _____ |

*Except as may otherwise be provided above for a particular contribution, contributions shall be paid in full or transferred and delivered to the partnership on or before*

_____.

## Interest on Contributed Capital

### Clause 9. No Interest Paid on Contributed Capital

*No partner shall be entitled to receive any interest on any capital contribution.*

### Clause 10. Interest Paid on Contributed Capital

*Each partner shall be entitled to interest on his or her capital contribution accruing at the rate of _____ percent per year from the date the contribution is paid. This interest shall be treated as an expense to be charged against income on the partnership books and shall be paid to the partner entitled to it on the following terms:*

_____.

# Failure To Make Contributions

### Clause 11. Failure To Contribute—Partnership Dissolves

*Except as otherwise provided in this agreement, if any partner fails to pay his or her initial contribution to the partnership by the date required by this agreement, the partnership shall immediately dissolve and each partner who has paid all or any portion of his or her initial contribution to the partnership's capital shall be entitled to a return of the funds and properties he or she contributed.*

### Clause 12.  Failure To Contribute— No Additional Contributions Required

*Except as otherwise provided in this agreement, if any partner fails to pay his or her contribution to the partnership capital as required by this agreement, the partnership shall not dissolve or terminate, but it shall continue as a partnership of only the partners who have made their initial capital contributions as required and without any partner who has failed to do so. In that case, the share in the partnership's profits and losses allocated under this agreement to any partner who has failed to make his or her initial contribution shall be reallocated to the remaining partners in proportion to their respective shares of partnership profits and losses as specified in this agreement.*

## Clause 13. Failure To Contribute—Additional Contributions Required

*Except as otherwise provided in this agreement, if any partner fails to pay his or her initial contributions to the partnership's capital as required by this agreement, the partnership shall not dissolve or terminate, but shall continue as a partnership of the partners who have made their initial capital contributions and without any partner who shall have failed to do so, but only if the remaining partners pay the initial capital contribution that was to have been made by the non-contributing partner or partners. The partnership shall promptly give written notice of this failure to all partners who have made their initial capital contributions. The notice shall specify the amount not paid. Within \_\_\_\_\_ days after the notice is given, the remaining partners shall pay the amount of the defaulted contribution in proportion to the respective amount they are required to pay to the partnership's capital under this agreement. That share of the profits of the partnership belonging to non-contributing partners shall then be reallocated to the remaining partner in proportion to their respective shares of separate property profits and losses under this agreement.*

## Clause 14. FailureTo Contribute Services

*If_____ fails to contribute the services as promised, the partnership shall proceed as follows:*

_____

# Future Contributions

### Clause 15. Future Contributions—If Approved by Unanimous Vote

*If, at any future time, more money is required to carry on the partnership business, and all of partners vote to increase the capital contributions required by partners, the additional capital shall be paid in by the partners as follows: _____*

### Clause 16. Future Contributions—Required Annually

*Each partner shall contribute annually _____ to the partnership's capital for a period of _____ years.*

# Loans to the Partnership

### Clause 17. Cash Loan

*_____ shall loan the partnership*
*_____ by _____*
*The partnership shall pay _____ percent interest on the loan.*

### Clause 18. Loan of Property

_____ *will loan to the partnership*
*the following item(s) of property:* _____
_____. *Each item of property lent to*
*the partnership shall remain the separate property of the lending partner*
*and shall be returned to that partner on the following terms:*

_____.

# Profits, Losses and Draws

## Profits and Losses

### Clause 19. Division of Profits and Losses

*The partnership profits and losses shall be shared among the partners as*
*follows:*

| Name of Partner | % of Profits | % of Losses |
|---|---|---|
| _____ | _____ | _____ |
| _____ | _____ | _____ |

### Clause 20. Date for Distribution of Profits

*Profits of the partnership shall be distributed in cash to the partners, in*
*proportion to their respective shares in the partnership's profits, in amounts*
*equal to the partnership's net profit for that period, according to the*
*following schedule:* _____.

# Restrictions on Payment of Profits

### Clause 21. Restriction on Payments—By Vote of Partners

*In determining the amount of profits available for distribution, allowance
will be made for the fact that some money must remain undistributed and
available as working capital, as determined by a vote of _____.*

### Clause 22. Restriction on Payments—According to Preset Formula

*The aggregate amounts distributed to the partners from the partnership
profits each year shall not exceed _____.*

# Draws to Partners

### Clause 23. Draws Authorized

*The following partners:*

*Names of Partners*

_____

_____

*are entitled to draws from expected partnership profits. The amount of each
draw will be determined by a vote of the partners . The draws shall be paid
according to the following terms: _____.*

### Clause 24. Draws Prohibited

*No partner shall be entitled to any draw against partnership profits, which shall be distributed only as provided in this agreement or by subsequent unanimous decision of the partners.*

### Clause 25. Draws Exceeding Profits Become Loans

*Notwithstanding the provisions of this agreement governing drawing permitted by partners, to the extent any partner's withdrawals for draws under those provisions during any fiscal year of the partnership exceed his or her share in the partnership's profits, the excess shall be regarded as a loan from the partnership to him or her that he or she is obligated to repay within _____ days after the end of that fiscal year.*

# Meeting and Voting Clauses

## Meetings of Partners

### Clause 26. Voting Power of Partners

*When making management decisions for the partnership, the partners shall have the following voting power:*

*Name of Partner*                            *Voting Power*

_____   _____

_____   _____

### Clause 27. Date and Place of Meetings

*The partners shall meet on _____*
*Other meetings of the partners can be called by a majority of the partners.*
*For such other meetings, each partner shall receive at least five working*
*days'o ral or written notice.*

## Voting Rules at Meetings

### Clause 28. Voting Rules—All Decisions Unanimous

*All partnership decisions must be made by the unanimous agreement of all*
*partners.*

### Clause 29. Voting Rules—Major Decisions Unanimous

*All major decisions of the partnership business must be made by a*
*unanimous decision of all partners. Minor business decisions may be made*
*by an individual partner. Major decisions are defined as:*

_____

### Clause 30. Voting Rule for Amendments to Agreement

*This agreement may only be amended by the vote of: _____*

_____

# Partners' Work Provisions

### Clause 31. Partners' Work Provisions

*The following provisions shall apply with respect to compensation, hours worked, skills to be contributed, sick leave, vacation time, and other matters regarding work performed by the partners for the partnership:*

_____.

# Financial Clauses

## Accountings

### Clause 32. Periodic Accountings Required

*Accountings of _____ shall be made every _____.*

### Clause 33. Annual Financial Statements Required

*A profit or net loss statement, together with other appropriate financial statements, shall be prepared as soon as practicable after the close of each fiscal year by the accountant or other tax advisor for the partnership.*

### Clause 34. Accounting Required Upon Request of Partner

*Accountings of any aspect of partnership business shall be made upon written request by any partner.*

# Expense Accounts

### Clause 35. Expense Accounts Authorized

*An expense account, not to exceed _____ per month, shall be set up for each partner for his or her actual, reasonable, and necessary expenses during the course of the business. Each partner shall keep an itemized record of these expenses and be reimbursed monthly on submission of the record.*

### Clause 36. Each Partner Pays Own Expenses

*The partners individually and personally shall assume and pay:*

*(a)   All expenses for the entertainment of persons doing business with the firm.*

*(b)   Expenses associated with usual business activities.*

# Other Financial Clauses

### Clause 37. Consent Required To Borrow Money

*A partner can borrow money on behalf of the partnership in excess of _____ only with prior consent of all partners.*

### Clause 38. Signatures Required on Partnership Checks

*All partnership funds shall be deposited in a bank or other financial institution in the name of the partnership and shall be subject to withdrawal only on the signatures of a least _____.*

### Clause 39. Maintenance of Financial Records

*Complete financial records of the partnership business shall be kept at the partnership's principal place of business and shall be open to inspection by any of the partners or their accredited representative at any reasonable time during business hours.*

### Clause 40. Deposit of Partnership Funds in Partnership Accounts

*All partnership funds shall be deposited only in bank accounts bearing the partnership name.*

### Clause 41. Authorization of a Client (Trust) Account

*All monies that do not belong to the partnership shall be deposited in a trust
account established in the partnership's name at _____
_____bank, and
shall be kept separate and not mingled with any other funds of the
partnership.*

# Outside Business Activities by Partners

### Clause 42. Outside Activities Permitted Except Direct Competition

*In addition to the business of the partnership, any partner may engage in
one or more other businesses, but only to the extent that this activity does
not directly and materially interfere with the business of the partnership
and does not conflict with the time commitments and other obligations of
that partner to the partnership under this agreement. Neither the
partnership nor any other partner shall have any right to any income or
profit derived by a partner from any business activity permitted under this
clause.*

### Clause 43. Specific Outside Activities by Partners Permitted

*The following are non-competing business activities that each partner plans
or may do outside the partnership business. Each partner is expressly
authorized to engage in these activities if he or she so desires:*

_____.

### Clause 44. Outside Activities by Partners Restricted

*As long as any person is a member of the partnership, he or she shall devote his or her full work time and energies to the conduct of partnership business, and shall not be actively engaged in the conduct of any other business for compensation or a share in profits as an employee, officer, agent, proprietor, partner, or stockholder. This prohibition shall not prevent him or her from being a passive investor in any enterprise, however, if he or she is not actively engaged in its business and does not exercise control over it. Neither the partnership nor any other partner shall have any right to any income or profit derived from any such passive investment.*

# Buy-Out Clauses

## Sale or Transfer of a Partner's Interest

### Clause 45. Sale of Departing Partner's Interest to Remaining Partners

*Except as otherwise provided in this agreement, if any partner leaves the partnership, for whatever reason, whether he or she quits, withdraws, is expelled, retires, becomes mentally or physically incapacitated to the extent that he or she is unable to function as a partner, or dies, then the partner, or his or her estate, personal representative, trustee, inheritors or other successors in interest, shall be obligated to sell the departing partner's interest in the partnership to the remaining partner or partners. The remaining partner or partners shall be entitled to buy that interest under the valuation method and other terms and conditions set forth in this agreement.*

## Clause 46. Partners' Refusal or Inability To Purchase Interest

*If the remaining partner or partners do not purchase the departing partner's share of the business according to the terms provided in this agreement, within _____ days after the departure of the partner, the entire business of the partnership shall be put up for sale and listed with the appropriate sales agencies, agents or brokers.*

## Clause 47. Offer To Purchase From Outsider

*If any partner receives a bona fide offer to purchase his or her interest in the partnership, and if the partner receiving the offer is willing to accept it, he or she shall give written notice of the amount and terms of the offer, the identity of the proposed buyer, and his or her willingness to accept the offer to each of the other partners. The other partner or partners shall have the option, within _____ days after the notice is given, to purchase that partner" interest on the same terms as those contained in the notice. If the remaining partner or partners do not exercise this option and purchase the departing partner's interest, the departing partner may sell his or her interest to the proposed buyer under the terms contained in the notice.*

## Conflicts Regarding Right To Buy a Departing Partner's Share

### Clause 48. Buy-Out Conflicts—Coin Flip

*If the partners cannot agree on who has the right to purchase the other partners' interest in the business, that right shall be determined by the flip of a coin as follows: _____.*

### Clause 49. Buy-Out Conflicts—Auction Bidding

*If the partners cannot agree who has the right to purchase the other partners' interest in the business, that right shall be determined by an auction, where each partner or group of partners shall bid on the business, with the right to raise their bids until one partner or group of partners drops out. The partner or group of partners eventually offering the highest bid shall have the right to buy the lower bidding partner's or group of partners's hares of the business. The buying partner or group shall pay for the purchased shares of the business under the terms provided in this agreement.*

## Buy-Out Valuation Clauses

### Clause 50. Market Value of Assets Valuation Method

*Except as otherwise provided in this agreement, the value of the partnership share of a departing partner shall be arrived at by determining the net worth of the partnership as of the date a partner leaves, for any reason. Net worth is defined as the market value, as of that date, of the following assets:*

1. *All tangible property, real or personal, owned by the business;*

2. *All the liquid assets owned by the business, including cash on hand, bank deposits and CDs or other moneys;*

3. *All accounts receivable;*

4. *All earned but unbilled fees;*

5. *All money presently earned for work in progress;*

*less the total amount of all debts owed by the business.*

## Clause 51. Partners Set Dollar Value of Partnership in Advance

*Except as otherwise provided in this agreement, the value of the partnership shall be determined as follows:*

1. *Within _____ days after the end of each fiscal year of the partnership, the partners shall determine the partnership's value by unanimous written agreement, and that value shall remain in effect from the date of that written determination until the next such written determination.*

2. *Should the partners be unable to agree on a value or otherwise fail to make any such determination, the partnership's value shall be the greater of (a) the value last established under this clause, or (b) _____*

*_____.*

## Clause 52. Capitalization of Earnings Valuation of Partnership

*Except as otherwise provided in this agreement, the value of the partnership shall be determined as follows:*

1. *The average yearly earnings of the business shall be calculated for the preceding _____.*

2. *"Earnings," as used in this clause, is defined as: _____.*

3. *The average yearly earnings shall then be multiplied by a multiple of _____ to give the value of the business, except as provided for in Section 4 of this clause, below.*

4. *In computing the value of the partnership under this agreement, the following factors shall be taken into account: _____ _____.*

## Clause 53. Insurance Proceeds Valuation Method

*Except as otherwise provided in this agreement, if a partner becomes disabled or dies, the value of his or her interest in the partnership, including the valuation for estate purposes, shall be the proceeds paid by the disability or life insurance policy maintained by the partnership or other partners for that partner according to the other terms of this agreement.*

## Clause 54. Post-Departure Appraisal Method

*Except as otherwise provided in this agreement, the value of the partnership shall be determined by an independent appraisal conducted, if possible, by _____. The appraisal shall be commenced within _____ days after the partner's departure from the partnership. The partnership and the departing partner shall share the cost of the appraisal equally.*

# Clauses Related to Buy-Outs

### Clause 55. Amount and Timing of Buy-Out Payments

*Except as otherwise provided in this agreement, whenever the partnership purchases a partner's interest, it shall pay for that interest according to the following terms: _____ .*

### Clause 56. Varying the Buy-Out Price in Special Circumstances

*The provisions in this agreement for calculating the value of the partnership, or for making payments to purchase the interest of a partner, shall be varied as follows, for the following reasons:*

*_____ .*

# Clauses Related to Departing Partners

### Clause 57. Partnership Continues after Departure of Partner

*In the case of a partner's death, permanent disability, retirement, voluntary withdrawal, expulsion from the partnership or death, the partnership shall not dissolve or terminate, but its business shall continue without interruption under the terms of this agreement.*

### Clause 58. Noncompetition for Departing Partners

*On the voluntary withdrawal, permanent disability, retirement, death or expulsion of any partner, that partner shall not carry on a business the same as or similar to the business of the partnership within _____ for a period of _____ .*

### Clause 59. Assumption of Departing Partner's Liabilities

*The continuing partnership shall pay, as they came due, all partnership debts and obligations that exist on the date a partner leaves the partnership, and shall hold the departing partner harmless from any claim arising from these debts and obligations.*

# Insurance and Estate Planning Clauses

## Insurance Policies

### Clause 60. Cross-Purchase of Insurance Policies by Partners

*Each partner shall purchase and maintain _____ insurance on the life of each other partner in the face value of _____ .*

### Clause 61. Partnership Purchases Insurance Policies

*The life insurance policies owned by the partnership on the lives of each partner are assets of the partnership only in so far as they have cash surrender value preceding the death of a partner.*

### Clause 62. Departing Partner Takes Over Insurance Policies

*On the withdrawal or termination of any partner for any reason other than his or her _____, any insurance policies on his or her _____ for which the partnership paid the premiums shall be delivered to that partner and become his or her separate property. If the policy has a cash surrender value, that amount shall be paid to the partnership by the withdrawing partner, or offset against the partnership's obligations to the withdrawing partner.*

## Control of the Business Name

### Clause 63. When Partner Departs—Partnership Owns Business Name

*The partnership business name of _____ is owned by the partnership. Should any partner cease to be a member of the partnership, the partnership shall continue to retain exclusive ownership and right to use the partnership business name.*

### Clause 64. When Partner Departs—Control of Name Decided Then

*The partnership business name of _____ is owned by the partnership. Should any person cease to be a partner and desire to use the partnership business name, and the remaining partners desire to continue the partnership and continue use of the partnership business name, ownership and control of the partnership business name shall be decided by _____.*

### Clause 65. When Partnership Dissolves—Majority Owns Name

*In the event of dissolution, the partnership business name of*
*_____ shall be owned by a majority of the*
*former partners. Any other former partner is not entitled to ownership or*
*use of the partnership business name.*

### Clause 66.  One Partner Owns Business Name
### on Departure or Dissolution

*The partnership business name of _____*
*shall be solely owned by _____ when he or*
*she ceases to be a partner or when the partnership dissolves.*

# Dispute Resolution Clauses

## Mediation

### Clause 67. Mediation

*The partners agree that except as otherwise provided in this agreement, any*
*dispute arising out of this agreement or the partnership business shall first*
*be resolved by mediation, if possible.*

*A partner who wishes to have a dispute mediated shall submit a written*
*request for mediation to each of the other partners. Mediation shall*
*commence within _____ days after the date of the partner's written request*
*for mediation.*

*The mediator shall be _____, if possible.*

*Any decision reached by mediation shall be reduced to writing, signed by all partners, and binding on them.*

*The costs of mediation shall be shared equally by all partners to the dispute.*

*The partners are aware that mediation is a voluntary process, and pledge to cooperate fully and fairly with the mediator in any attempt to reach a mutually satisfactory compromise to a dispute. If, after a good faith effort by a partner to participate in the mediation process, a partner feels the dispute cannot be resolved, he or she shall so notify the other partners, and the mediator, in writing.*

*If the partners fail to resolve the dispute by mediation, the dispute shall be arbitrated as may be provided in a separate arbitration clause in this agreement.*

# Arbitration

## Clause 68. Arbitration With One Arbitrator

*The partners agree that, except as otherwise provided in this agreement, any dispute arising out of this agreement, or the partnership business, shall be arbitrated under the terms of this clause.*

*The arbitration shall be carried out by a single arbitrator who shall be _____. If this person is unwilling or unable to act as arbitrator, then the following alternate arbitrator, or procedure to select an alternate arbitrator, shall be used:*

*_____.*

*Any arbitration shall be held as follows:*

1. *The partner(s) initiating the arbitration procedure shall inform the other partner(s) in writing of the nature of the dispute at the same time that he or she notifies the arbitrator.*

2. *Within _____ days from receipt of this notice, the other partners shall reply in writing, stating their views of the nature of the dispute.*

3. *The arbitrator shall hold a hearing on the dispute within seven days after the reply of the other partner(s). Each partner shall be entitled to present whatever oral or written statements he or she wishes and may present witnesses at the hearing.*

4. *The arbitrator shall make his or her decision in writing.*

5. *If the partner(s) to whom the demand for arbitration is directed fails to respond within the proper time limit, the partner(s) initiating the arbitration must give the other an additional five days' written notice of "intention to proceed to arbitration." If there is still no response, the partner(s) initiating the arbitration may proceed with the arbitration before the arbitrator, and his or her award shall be binding.*

6. *The cost of arbitration shall be borne by the partners as the arbitrator directs.*

7. *The arbitration award shall be conclusive and binding on the partners and shall be set forth in such a way that a formal judgment can be entered in the court having jurisdiction over the dispute if either party so desires.*

## Clause 69. Arbitration With Three Arbitrators

*The partners agree that, except as otherwise provided in this agreement, any dispute arising out of this agreement or the partnership business shall be arbitrated under the terms of this clause. The arbitration shall be carried out by three arbitrators. Each partner or side to the dispute shall appoint* one arbitrator. The two designated arbitrators shall appoint the third arbitrator.

The arbitration shall be carried out as follows:

1. The partner(s) initiating the arbitration procedure shall inform the other partner(s) in writing of the nature of the dispute at the same time that they designate one arbitrator.

2. Within _____ days from receipt of this notice, the other partners shall reply in writing naming the second arbitrator, and stating their view of the nature of the dispute.

3. The two designated arbitrators shall name a third arbitrator within ten days from the date the second arbitrator is named. If they cannot agree, the following procedure shall be used to name the third arbitrator:

   _____.

4. An arbitration meeting shall be held within _____ days after the third arbitrator is named.

5. Each partner shall be entitled to present whatever oral or written statements he or she wishes and may present witnesses at the arbitration meeting.

6. The arbitrators shall make their decision in writing.

7. If the partner(s) to whom the demand for arbitration is directed fails to respond within the proper time limit, the partner(s) initiating the arbitration must give the other an additional five days' written notice of "intention to proceed to arbitration." If there is still no response, the partner(s) initiating the arbitration may proceed with the arbitration before the arbitrators, and their award shall be binding.

8. The cost of arbitration shall be borne by the partners as the arbitrators shall direct.

9. *The arbitration award shall be conclusive and binding on the partners and shall be set forth in such a way that a formal judgment can be entered in the court having jurisdiction over the dispute if either party so desires.*

# Expulsion of Partner Clauses

## Clause 70. Procedure and Grounds for Expulsion

*A partner may be expelled from the partnership as follows:*

---

*Expulsion shall become effective when written notice of expulsion is received by the expelled partner. When the expulsion becomes effective, the expelled partner's right to participate in the partnership's profits and his or her other rights, powers and authority as a partner of the partnership shall terminate. An expelled partner shall be entitled to receive the value of his or her interest in the partnership according to the provisions of this agreement.*

## Clause 71. Expulsion of a Partner for Bankruptcy

*Notwithstanding any other provision of this agreement, a partner shall cease to be a partner and shall have no interest in common with the remaining partners or in partnership property when the partner does any of the following:*

1. *Seeks protection of the U.S. Bankruptcy Court under Chapter 7, Chapter 11 or other provisions of the federal Bankruptcy Code.*

2. *Obtains or becomes subject to an order or decree of insolvency under state law.*

3. *Makes an assignment for the benefit of creditors.*

4. *Consents to or accepts the appointment of a receiver or trustee to any substantial part of his or her assets that is not vacated within _____ days.*

5. *Consents to or accepts an attachment or execution of any substantial part of his or her assets that's not released within _____ days.*

*From the date of any of the preceding events, the partner shall be considered as a seller to the partnership of his or her interest in the partnership and shall be entitled to receive the value of his or her interest in the partnership according to the provisions of this agreement. If a partner is expelled under the terms of this clause, the partnership shall not be dissolved, but shall continue to function without interruption.*

# Admission of New Partners

## Clause 72. Admission of New Partners—By Unanimous Consent

*A new partner or partners may be added to this partnership only by the unanimous written agreement of all existing partners.*

## Clause 73. Admission of New Partners—By Less Than All Partners

*A new partner may be admitted to the partnership with the written approval of: _____.*

### Clause 74. No Dissolution When New Partner Admitted

*Admission of a new partner or partners shall not cause dissolution of the partnership business.*

## Incoming Partner's Liability for Partnership Debts

### Clause 75.  New Partner Liable for Existing Debts Up to Capital Contribution

*The undersigned partner, _____,
expressly assumes personal liability for debts of the partnership incurred on
or before _____ equal to the amount of his
or her contribution to the partnership, totaling _____.*

### Clause 76. New Partner Liable for New Debts Only

*The undersigned partner, _____, shall
not be personally responsible for, or assume any liability for, any debts of
the partnership incurred before _____.*

### Clause 77. New Partner Liable for All Debts

*The undersigned partner, _____, hereby
expressly assumes full personal liability for the past, present and future
debts of the partnership.*

# Additional Provisions

## Clause 78. Additional Provisions

*Insert any additional partnership agreement clause in this space:*

_____.

# Standard Clauses

## Clause 79. State Law

*The partners have formed this general partnership under the laws of the State of _____, intending to be legally bound thereby.*

## Clause 80. Attachments to Agreement

*Any sheet or document referred to in and attached to, or included with, this partnership agreement shall be regarded as fully contained in this partnership agreement.*

## Clause 81. Agreement Is Entire Understanding of Partners

*This agreement contains the entire understanding of the partners regarding their rights and duties in the partnership. This agreement may not be orally modified under any circumstances. Further, a written modification shall only be effective if properly approved and signed by the partners as an amendment to this agreement under the terms of this agreement.*

## Clause 82. Agreement Is Binding on Successors

*This agreement shall be binding on and for the benefit of the successors, inheritors, assigns and personal representatives of the partners, except to the extent of any contrary provision in the agreement.*

## Clause 83. Agreement Stands if Clause Is Invalidated

*If any term, provision, or condition of this agreement is held by a court of competent jurisdiction to be invalid, void or unenforceable, the rest of the agreement shall remain in full force and effect and shall in no way be affected, impaired or invalidated.*

## Clause 84. Spousal Consent

*The following spouse(s) of the partners has (have) read and understand this partnership agreement and consent(s) to all clauses and terms in it. The spouse(s) also specifically agree(s) that the business valuation method contained in the agreement shall be used in any legal proceeding to determine the value of any interest the spouse(s) may have in the business.*

_____

*Signature(s) of Spouse(s)*

# B. SAMPLE.DOC Clauses

PARTNERSHIP AGREEMENT

## I. NAMES OF THE PARTNERS AND EFFECTIVE DATE

This partnership agreement is entered into and effective as of _____, by:

NAME OF PARTNER: _____

NAME OF PARTNER: _____

the partners.

## II. NAME OF THE PARTNERSHIP

The name of the partnership is _____.

## III. NAME OF THE BUSINESS

The name of the partnership business is _____

## IV. TERM—UNTIL DISSOLUTION OF PARTNERSHIP

The partnership shall last until it is dissolved by all the partners or according to the terms of this agreement.

## V. PURPOSES OF THE PARTNERSHIP

The purposes of the partnership are: _____.

## VI. CONTRIBUTIONS

The following persons shall make the following contributions of cash property or services to the partnership in return for the following ownership shares in the partnership:

NAME OF PARTNER: _____

DESCRIPTION OF CONTRIBUTION: _____

PERCENTAGE: _____

NAME OF PARTNER: _____

DESCRIPTION OF CONTRIBUTION: _____

PERCENTAGE: _____

Except as may otherwise be provided above for a particular contribution, contributions shall be paid in full or transferred and delivered to the partnership on or before

_____.

## VII. DIVISION OF PROFITS AND LOSSES

The partnership profits and losses shall be shared among the partners as follows:

NAME OF PARTNER: _____

% OF PROFITS: _____

% OF LOSSES: _____

NAME OF PARTNER: _____

% OF PROFITS: _____

% OF LOSSES: _____

## VIII. VOTING POWER OF PARTNERS

When making management decisions for the partnership, the partners shall have the following voting power:

NAME OF PARTNER: _____

VOTING POWER: _____

NAME OF PARTNER: _____

VOTING POWER: _____

## IX. DATE AND PLACE OF MEETINGS

The partners shall meet on _____. Other meetings of the partners can be called by a majority of the partners. For such other meetings, each partner shall receive at least five working days' oral or written notice.

## X. VOTING RULES—ALL DECISIONS UNANIMOUS

All partnership decisions must be made by the unanimous agreement of all partners.

## XI. SALE OF DEPARTING PARTNER'S INTEREST TO REMAINING PARTNERS

Except as otherwise provided in this agreement, if any partner leaves the partnership, for whatever reason, whether he or she quits, withdraws, is expelled, retires, becomes mentally or physically incapacitated to the extent that he or she is unable to function as a partner or dies, then the partner, or his or her estate, personal representative, trustee, inheritors or other successors in interest, shall be obligated to sell the departing partner's interest in the partnership to the remaining partner or partners. The remaining partner or partners shall be entitled to buy that interest under the valuation method and other terms and conditions set forth in this agreement.

## XII. PARTNERS' REFUSAL OR INABILITY TO PURCHASE INTEREST

If the remaining partner or partners do not purchase the departing partner's share of the business according to the terms provided in this agreement, within _____days after the departure of the partner, the entire business of the partnership shall be put up for sale and listed with the appropriate sales agencies, agents or brokers.

## XIII. MARKET VALUE OF ASSETS VALUATION METHOD

Except as otherwise provided in this agreement, the value of the partnership share of a departing partner shall be arrived at by determining the net worth of the partnership as of the date a partner leaves, for any reason. Net worth is defined as the market value, as of that date, of the following assets:

1. All tangible property, real or personal, owned by the business;

2. All liquid assets owned by the business, including cash on hand, bank deposits, CDs, money market funds or other monies;

3. All accounts receivable;

4. All earned but unbilled fees;

5. All money presently earned for work in progress;

less the total amount of all debts owed by the business.

## XIV. AMOUNT AND TIMING OF BUY-OUT PAYMENTS

Except as otherwise provided in this agreement, when the partnership purchases a partner's interest, it shall pay for that interest according to the following terms:

_____.

## XV. MEDIATION

The partners agree that except as otherwise provided in this agreement, any dispute arising out of this agreement or the partnership business shall first be resolved by mediation, if possible.

A partner who wishes to have a dispute mediated shall submit a written request for mediation to each of the other partners. Mediation shall commence within _____ days after the date of the partner's written request for mediation.

The mediator shall be _____, if possible.

Any decision reached by mediation shall be reduced to writing, signed by all partners, and binding on them.

The costs of mediation shall be shared equally by all partners to the dispute.

The partners are aware that mediation is a voluntary process, and pledge to cooperate fully and fairly with the mediator in any attempt to reach a mutually satisfactory compromise to a dispute. If, after a good faith effort by a partner to participate in the mediation process, a partner feels the dispute cannot be resolved, he or she shall so notify the other partners, and the mediator, in writing.

If the partners cannot resolve the dispute by mediation, the dispute shall be arbitrated as may be provided in a separate arbitration clause in this agreement.

## XVI. ARBITRATION WITH ONE ARBITRATOR

The partners agree that, except as otherwise provided in this agreement, any dispute arising out of this agreement, or the partnership business, shall be arbitrated under the terms of this clause.

The arbitration shall be carried out by a single arbitrator who shall be _____ If this person is unwilling or unable to act as arbitrator, then the following alternate arbitrator, or procedure to select an alternate arbitrator, shall be used: _____.

Any arbitration shall be held as follows:

1. The partner(s) initiating the arbitration procedure shall inform the other partner(s) in writing of the nature of the dispute at the same time that he or she notifies the arbitrator.

2. Within _____ days from receipt of this notice, the other partners shall reply in writing, stating their views of the nature of the dispute.

3. The arbitrator shall hold a hearing on the dispute within seven days after the reply of the other partner(s). Each partner shall be entitled to present whatever oral or written statements he or she wishes and may present witnesses at the hearing.

4. The arbitrator shall make his or her decision in writing.

5. If the partner(s) to whom the demand for arbitration is directed fails to respond within the proper time limit, the partner(s) initiating the arbitration must give the other an

additional five days' written notice of "intention to proceed to arbitration." If there is still no response, the partner(s) initiating the arbitration may proceed with the arbitration before the arbitrator, and his or her award shall be binding.

6. The cost of arbitration shall be borne by the partners as the arbitrator directs.

7. The arbitration award shall be conclusive and binding on the partners and shall be set forth in such a way that a formal judgment can be entered in the court having jurisdiction over the dispute if either party so desires.

## XVII. ADMISSION OF NEW PARTNERS—BY UNANIMOUS CONSENT

A new partner or partners may be added to this partnership only by the unanimous written agreement of all existing partners.

## XVIII. STATE LAW

The partners have formed this general partnership under the laws of the State of _____, intending to be legally bound thereby.

## XIX. ATTACHMENTS TO AGREEMENT

Any sheet or document referred to in and attached to, or included with, this partnership agreement shall be regarded as fully contained in this partnership agreement.

## XX. AGREEMENT IS ENTIRE UNDERSTANDING OF PARTNERS

This agreement contains the entire understanding of the partners regarding their rights and duties in the partnership. This agreement may not be orally modified under any circumstances. Further, a written modification shall only be effective if properly approved and signed by the partners as an amendment to this agreement under the terms of this agreement.

## XXI. AGREEMENT IS BINDING ON SUCCESSORS

This agreement shall be binding on and for the benefit of the successors, inheritors, assigns and personal representatives of the partners, except to the extent of any contrary provision in the agreement.

## XXII. AGREEMENT STANDS IF CLAUSE IS INVALIDATED

If any term, provision or condition of this agreement is held by a court of competent jurisdiction to be invalid, void or unenforceable, the rest of the agreement shall remain in full force and effect and shall in no way be affected, impaired or invalidated.

## XXII. PARTNERS' SIGNATURES

Signed By: _____:_____

Dated: _____

Signed By: _____:_____

Dated: _____

The following spouse(s) of the partners have read and understand this partnership agreement and consent(s) to all clauses and terms in it. The undersigned spouse(s) also specifically agree that the business valuation method contained in the agreement shall be used in any legal proceeding to determine the value of any interest the spouse(s) may have in the business.

Spouse's Signature: _____

Dated: _____

Spouse's Signature: _____

Dated: _____

# C. List of State Uniform Partnership Act Laws

| State | Statutory Citation |
|---|---|
| Alabama | Code 1975, §§ 10-8-1 to 10-8-103. |
| Alaska | AS 32.05.010 to 32.05.430. |
| Arizona | A.R.S. §§ 29-201 to 29-244. |
| Arkansas | A.C.A. §§ 4-42-101 to 4-42-702. |
| California | West's Ann.Cal.Corp.Code §§ 15001 to 15045. |
| Colorado | C.R.S. 7-60-101 to 7-60-143. |
| Connecticut | C.G.S.A. §§ 34-39 to 34-82. |
| Delaware | 6 Del.C. §§ 1501 to 1543. |
| District of Columbia | D.C. Code 1981, §§ 41-101 to 41-142. |
| Florida | West's F.S.A. §§ 620.56 to 620.77. |
| Georgia | O.C.G.A. §§ 14-8-1 to 14-8-43. |
| Hawaii | HRS §§ 425-101 to 425-143. |
| Idaho | I.C. §§ 53-301 to 53-343. |
| Illinois | S.H.A. ch. 106-1/2, §§ 1 to 43. |
| Indiana | West's A.I.C. 23-4-1-1 to 23-4-1-43. |
| Iowa | I.C.A. §§ 544.1 to 544.43. |
| Kansas | K.S.A. 56-301 to 56-343. |
| Kentucky | KRS 362.150 to 362.360. |
| Maine | 31 M.R.S.A. §§ 281 to 323. |
| Maryland | Code, Corporations and Associations, §§ 9-101 to 9-703. |
| Massachusetts | M.G.L.A. ch. 108A, §§ 1 to 44. |
| Michigan | M.C.L.A. §§ 449.1 to 449.43. |
| Minnesota | M.S.A. §§ 323.01 to 323.43. |
| Mississippi | Code 1972, §§ 79-12-1 to 79-12-85. |
| Missouri | V.A.M.S. §§ 358.010 to 358.430. |
| Montana | MCA 35-10-101 to 35-10-615. |
| Nebraska | R.R.S. 1943, §§ 67-301 to 67-343. |
| Nevada | N.R.S. 87.010 to 87.430. |
| New Hampshire | RSA 304-A:1 to 304-A:43. |
| New Jersey | N.J.S.A. 42:1-1 to 42:1-43. |
| New Mexico | NMSA 1978, §§ 54-1-1 to 54-1-43. |
| New York | McKinney's Partnership Law, §§ 1 to 74. |
| North Carolina | G.S. §§ 59-31 to 59-73. |
| North Dakota | NDCC 45-05-01 to 45-09-15, 45-12-04. |
| Ohio | R.C. §§ 1775.01 to 1775.42. |
| Oklahoma | 54 Okl.St.Ann. §§ 201 to 243. |
| Oregon | ORS 68.010 to 68.650. |
| Pennsylvania | 15 Pa.C.S.A. §§ 8301 to 8365. |
| Rhode Island | Gen.Laws 1956, §§ 7-12-12 to 7-12-55. |
| South Carolina | Code 1976, §§ 33-41-10 to 33-41-1090. |
| South Dakota | SDCL 48-1-1 to 48-5-56. |
| Tennessee | T.C.A. §§ 61-1-101 to 61-1-142. |
| Texas | Vernon's Ann.Texas Civ. St. art. 6132b. |
| Utah | U.C.A. 1953, 48-1-1 to 48-1-40. |
| Vermont | 11 V.S.A. §§ 1121 to 1335. |
| Virginia | Code 1950, §§ 50-1 to 50-43. |
| Washington | West's RCWA 25.04.010 to 25.04.430. |
| West Virginia | Code, 47-8A-1 to 47-8A-45. |
| Wisconsin | W.S.A. 178.01 to 178.39. |

# CATALOG

## ESTATE PLANNING & PROBATE

### Plan Your Estate With a Living Trust
*Attorney Denis Clifford*
*National 2nd Edition*
This book covers every significant aspect of estate planning and gives detailed specific, instructions for preparing a living trust, a document that lets your family avoid expensive and lengthy probate court proceedings after your death. *Plan Your Estate* includes all the tear-out forms and step-by-step instructions to let you prepare an estate plan designed for your special needs.
**$19.95/NEST**

### Nolo's Simple Will Book
*Attorney Denis Clifford*
*National 2nd Edition*
It's easy to write a legally valid will using this book. The instructions and forms enable people to draft a will for all needs, including naming a personal guardian for minor children, leaving property to minor children or young adults and updating a will when necessary. Good in all states except Louisiana.
**$17.95/SWIL**

### How to Probate an Estate
*Julia Nissley*
*California 6th Edition*
If you find yourself responsible for winding up the legal and financial affairs of a deceased family member or friend, you can often save costly attorneys' fees by handling the probate process yourself. This book also explains the simple procedures you can use to transfer assets that don't require probate, including property held in joint tenancy or living trusts or as community property.
**$34.95/PAE**

## software

### WillMaker
*Nolo Press*
*Version 4.0*
This easy-to-use software program lets you prepare and update a legal will—safely, privately and without the expense of a lawyer. Leading you step-by-step in a question-and-answer format, *WillMaker* builds a will around your answers, taking into account your state of residence. *WillMaker* comes with a 200-page legal manual which provides the legal background necessary to make sound choices. Good in all states except Louisiana.
**IBM PC**
**(31/2 & 51/4 disks included)**
**$69.95/WI4**
**MACINTOSH $69.95/WM4**

### Nolo's Personal RecordKeeper
*(formerly For the Record)*

*Carol Pladsen & Attorney Ralph Warner*
*Version 3.0*
*Nolo's Personal RecordKeeper* lets you record the location of personal, financial and legal information in over 200 categories and subcategories. It also allows you to create lists of insured property, compute net worth, consolidate emergency information into one place and export to *Quicken®* home inventory and net worth reports. Includes a 320-page manual filled with practical and legal advice.
**IBM PC**
**(3-1/2 & 5-1/4 disks included)**
**$49.95/FRI3**
**MACINTOSH $49.95/FRM3**

### Nolo's Living Trust
*Attorney Mary Randolph*
*Version 1.0*

A will is an indispensable part of any estate plan, but many people need a living trust as well. By putting certain assets into a trust, you save your heirs the headache, time and expense of probate. *Nolo's Living Trust* lets you set up an individual or shared marital trust, make your trust document legal, transfer your property to the trust, and change or revoke the trust at any time. Includes on-line legal help screens, glossary and a 380-page manual that guides you through the process. Good in all states except Louisiana.
**MACINTOSH $79.95/LTM1**

## GOING TO COURT

### Everybody's Guide to Municipal Court
*Judge Roderic Duncan*
*California 1st Edition*
*Everybody's Guide to Municipal Court* explains how to prepare and defend the most common types of contract and personal injury law suits in California Municipal Court. It provides step-by-step instructions for preparing and filing all necessary forms, gathering evidence and appearing in court.
**$29.95/MUNI**

### Fight Your Ticket
*Attorney David Brown*
*California 5th Edition*
This book shows you how to fight an unfair traffic ticket—when you're stopped, at arraignment, at trial and on appeal.
**$17.95/FYT**

### Collect Your Court Judgment
*Gini Graham Scott, Attorney Stephen Elias & Lisa Goldoftas*
*California 2nd Edition*
This book contains step-by-step instructions and all the forms you need to collect a court judgment from the debtor's bank accounts, wages, business receipts, real estate or other assets.
**$19.95/JUDG**

### Everybody's Guide to Small Claims Court
*Attorney Ralph Warner*
*National 5th Edition*
*California 10th Edition*
These books will help you decide if you should sue in Small Claims Court, show you how to file and serve papers, tell you what to bring to court and how to collect a judgment.
**National $15.95/NSCC**
**California $15.95/ CSCC**

### How to Change Your Name
*Attorneys David Loeb & David Brown*
*California 5th Edition*
This book explains how to change your name legally and provides all the necessary court forms with detailed instructions on how to fill them out.
**$19.95/NAME**

### The Criminal Records Book
*Attorney Warren Siegel*
*California 3rd Edition*
This book shows you step-by-step how to seal criminal records, dismiss convictions, destroy marijuana records and reduce felony convictions.
**$19.95/CRIM**

### The Legal Guide for Starting & Running a Small Business
*Attorney Fred S. Steingold*
*National 1st Edition*
This is an essential resource for every small business owner. Find out everything you need to know about how to form a sole proprietorship, partnership or corporation, negotiate a favorable lease, hire and fire employees, write contracts and resolve business disputes.
**$19.95 / RUNS**

### Sexual Harassment on the Job
*Attorneys William Petrocelli & Barbara Kate Repa*
*National 1st Edition*
This is the first comprehensive book dealing with sexual harassment in the workplace. It describes what harassment is, what the laws are that make it illegal and how to put a stop to it. This guide is invaluable both for employees experiencing harassment and for employers interested in creating a policy against sexual harassment and a procedure for handling complaints.
**$14.95/HARS**

### Your Rights in the Workplace
*Dan Lacey*
*National 1st Edition*
*Your Rights in the Workplace,* the first comprehensive guide to workplace rights—from hiring to firing—explains the latest sweeping changes in laws passed to protect workers. Learning about these legal protections can help all workers be sure they're paid fairly and on time, get all employment benefits, and know how to take action if fired or laid off illegally.
**$15.95/YRW**

### How to Write a Business Plan
*Mike McKeever*
*National 4th Edition*
If you're thinking of starting a business or raising money to expand an existing one, this book will show you how to write the business plan and loan package necessary to finance your business and make it work.
**$19.95/SBS**

### Marketing Without Advertising
*Michael Phillips & Salli Rasberry*
*National 1st Edition*
This book outlines practical steps for building and expanding a small business without spending a lot of money on advertising.
**$14.00/MWAD**

### The Partnership Book
*Attorneys Denis Clifford & Ralph Warner*
*National 4th Edition*
This book shows you step-by-step how to write a solid partnership agreement that meets your needs. It covers initial contributions to the business, wages, profit-sharing, buy-outs, death or retirement of a partner and disputes.
**$24.95/PART**

### How to Form Your Own Nonprofit Corporation
*Attorney Anthony Mancuso*
*National 1st Edition*
This book explains the legal formalities involved and provides detailed information on the differences in the law among 50 states. It also contains forms for the Articles, Bylaws and Minutes you need, along with complete instructions for obtaining federal 501 (c) (3) tax exemptions and qualifying for public charity status.
**$24.95/NNP**

### The California Nonprofit Corporation Handbook
*Attorney Anthony Mancuso*
*California 6th Edition*
This book shows you step-by-step how to form and operate a nonprofit corporation in California. It includes the latest corporate and tax law changes, and the forms for the Articles, Bylaws and Minutes.
**$29.95/NON**

### How to Form Your Own Corporation
*Attorney Anthony Mancuso*
*California 7th Edition*
*New York 2nd Edition*
*Texas 4th Edition*
*Florida 3rd Edition*
These books contain the forms, instructions and tax information you need to incorporate a small business yourself and save hundreds of dollars in lawyers' fees.
**California $29.95/CCOR**
**New York $24.95/NYCO**
**Texas $29.95/TCOR**
**Florida $24.95/FLCO**

### The California Professional Corporation Handbook
*Attorney Anthony Mancuso*
*California 4th Edition*
Health care professionals, lawyers, accountants and members of certain other professions must fulfill special requirements when forming a corporation in California. This book contains up-to-date tax information plus all the forms and instructions necessary to form a California professional corporation.
**$34.95/PROF**

## The Independent Paralegal's Handbook

*Attorney Ralph Warner*
*National 2nd Edition*
*The Independent Paralegal's Handbook* provides legal and business guidelines for those who want to take routine legal work out of the law office and offer it for a reasonable fee in an independent business.
**$19.95/ PARA**

## Getting Started as an Independent Paralegal

*(Two Audio Tapes)*
*Attorney Ralph Warner*
*National 2nd Edition*
If you are interested in going into business as an Independent Paralegal —helping consumers prepare their own legal paperwork—you'll want to listen to these tapes. Approximately two hours in length, the tapes will tell you everything you need to know about what legal tasks to handle, how much to charge and how to run a profitable business.
**$44.95/GSIP**

## Nolo's Partnership Maker

*Attorney Tony Mancuso &*
*Michael Radtke*
*Version 1.0*
*Nolo's Partnership Maker* prepares a legal partnership agreement for doing business in any state. The program can be used by anyone who plans to pool energy, efforts, money or property with others in any type of mutual endeavor. You can select and assemble the standard partnership clauses provided or create your own customized agreement.thatcan be updated at any time. Includes on-line legal help screens, glossary and tutorial, and a manual that takes you through the process step-by-step.
**IBM PC**
**(3-1/2 & 5-1/4 disks included)**
**$129.00/PAGI1**

## California Incorporator

*Attorney Anthony Mancuso*
*Version 1.0 (good only in CA)*

Answer the questions on the screen and this software program will print out the 35-40 pages of documents you need to make your California corporation legal. Comes with a 200-page manual which explains the incorporation process.
**IBM PC**
**(3-1/2 & 5-1/4 disks included)**
**$129.00/INCI**

## The California Nonprofit Corporation Handbook

*(computer edition)*
*Attorney Anthony Mancuso*
*Version 1.0 (good only in CA)*
This book/software package shows you step-by-step how to form and operate a nonprofit corporation in California. Included on disk are the forms for the Articles, Bylaws and Minutes.
**IBM PC 5-1/4  $69.95/ NPI**
**IBM PC 3-1/2  $69.95/ NP3I**
**MACINTOSH $69.95/ NPM**

## How to Form Your Own New York Corporation & How to Form Your Own Texas Corporation

*(computer editions)*
*Attorney Anthony Mancuso*
These book/software packages contain the instructions and tax information and forms you need to incorporate a small business and save hundreds of dollars in lawyers' fees. All organizational forms are on disk. Both come with a 250-page manual.
**New York 1st Edition**
**IBM PC 5-1/4  $69.95/ NYCI**
**IBM PC 3-1/2  $69.95/ NYC3I**
**MACINTOSH $69.95/ NYCM**

**Texas 1st Edition**
**IBM PC 5-1/4  $69.95/ TCI**
**IBM PC 3-1/2  $69.95/ TC3I**
**MACINTOSH $69.95/ TCM**

## Dog Law

*Attorney Mary Randolph*
*National 1st Edition*
*Dog Law* is a practical guide to the laws that affect dog owners and their neighbors. You'll find answers to common questions on such topics as biting, barking, veterinarians and more.
**$12.95/DOG**

## Neighbor Law: Fences, Trees, Boundaries & Noise

*Attorney Cora Jordan*
*National 1st Edition*
*Neighbor Law* answers common questions about the subjects that most often trigger disputes between neighbors: fences, trees, boundaries and noise. It explains how to find the law and resolve disputes without a nasty lawsuit.
**$14.95/NEI**

## Stand Up to the IRS

*Attorney Fred Daily*
*National 1st Edition*
*Stand Up to the IRS* gives detailed stategies on surviving an audit with the minimum amount of damage, appealing an audit decision, going to Tax Court and dealing with IRS collectors. It also discusses filing tax returns when you haven't done so in a while, tax crimes, concerns of small business people and getting help from the IRS ombudsman.
**$19.95 / SUIRS**

## Barbara Kaufman's Consumer Action Guide

*Barbara Kaufman*
*California 1st Edition*
This practical handbook is filled with information on hundreds of consumer topics. It gives consumers access to their legal rights, providing addresses and phone numbers of where to complain when things go wrong, and providing resources if more help is necessary.
**$14.95/CAG**

## Money Troubles: Legal Strategies to Cope With Your Debts

*Attorney Robin Leonard*
*National 1st Edition*

Are you behind on your credit card bills or loan payments? If you are, then *Money Troubles* is exactly what you need. It covers everything from knowing what your rights are, and asserting them, to helping you evaluate your individual situation. This practical, straightforward book is for anyone who needs help understanding and dealing with the complex and often scary topic of debts.
**$16.95/MT**

## How To File for Bankruptcy

*Attorneys Stephen Elias, Albin Renauer & Robin Leonard*
*National 3rd Edition*

Trying to decide whether or not filing for bankruptcy makes sense? *How to File for Bankruptcy* contains an overview of the process and all the forms plus step-by-step instructions on the procedures to follow.
**$24.95/HFB**

## Simple Contracts for Personal Use

*Attorney Stephen Elias & Marcia Stewart*
*National 2nd Edition*

This book contains clearly written legal form contracts to buy and sell property, borrow and lend money, store and lend personal property, release others from personal liability, or pay a contractor to do home repairs. Includes agreements to arrange childcare and other household help.
**$16.95/CONT**

## Divorce & Money

*Violet Woodhouse & Victoria Felton-Collins with M.C. Blakeman*
*National 1st Edition*

*Divorce & Money* explains how to evaluate such major assets as family homes and businesses, investments, pensions, and how to arrive at a division of property that is fair to both sides. Throughout, the book emphasizes the difference between legal reality—how the court evaluates assets, and financial reality—what the assets are really worth.
**$19.95/DIMO**

## The Living Together Kit

*Attorneys Toni Ihara & Ralph Warner*
*National 6th Edition*

*The Living Together Kit* is a detailed guide designed to help the increasing number of unmarried couples living together understand the laws that affect them. Sample agreements and instructions are included.
**$17.95/LTK**

## A Legal Guide for Lesbian and Gay Couples

*Attorneys Hayden Curry & Denis Clifford*
*National 6th Edition*

Laws designed to regulate and protect unmarried couples don't apply to lesbian and gay couples. This book shows you step-by-step how to write a living-together contract, plan for medical emergencies, and plan your estates. Includes forms, sample agreements and lists of both national lesbian and gay legal organizations and AIDS organizations.
**$17.95/LG**

## Trademark: How To Name Your Business & Product

*Attorneys Kate McGrath and Stephen Elias, With Trademark Attorney Sarah Shena*
*National 1st Edition*

*Trademark: How to Name Your Business & Product* explains step-by-step how to protect names used to market services and products. Especially designed for small businesses, the book shows how to: choose a name or logo that others can't copy, conduct a trademark search, register a trademark with the U.S. Patent and Trademark Office and protect and maintain the trademark.
**$29.95 / TRD**

## Patent It Yourself

*Attorney David Pressman*
*National 3rd Edition*

From the patent search to the actual application, this book covers everything including the use and licensing of patents, successful marketing and how to deal with infringement.
**$34.95/PAT**

## The Inventor's Notebook

*Fred Grissom & Attorney David Pressman*
*National 1st Edition*

This book helps you document the process of successful independent inventing by providing forms, instructions, references to relevant areas of patent law, a bibliography of legal and non-legal aids and more.
**$19.95/INOT**

## The Copyright Handbook

*Attorney Stephen Fishman*
*National 1st Edition*

Anyone who works with words needs to know about copyright laws. This book provides forms and step-by-step instructions for protecting all types of written expression under U.S. and international copyright law. It contains detailed reference chapters on such major copyright-related topics as copyright infringement, fair use, works for hire and transfers of copyright ownership.
**$24.95/COHA**

## How to Copyright Software

*Attorney M.J. Salone*
*National 3rd Edition*
This book tells you how to register your copyright for maximum protection and discusses who owns a copyright on software developed by more than one person.
**$39.95/COPY**

## HOMEOWNERS

## How to Buy a House in California

*Attorney Ralph Warner, Ira Serkes*
*& George Devine*
*California 2nd Edition*
This book shows you how to find a house, work with a real estate agent, make an offer and negotiate intelligently. Includes information on all types of mortgages as well as private financing options.
**$19.95/BHCA**

## The Deeds Book

*Attorney Mary Randolph*
*California 2nd Edition*
If you own real estate, you'll need to sign a new deed when you transfer the property or put it in trust as part of your estate planning. This book shows you how to find the right kind of deed, complete the tear-out forms and record them in the county recorder's public records.
**$15.95/DEED**

## For Sale By Owner

*George Devine*
*California 2nd Edition*
*For Sale By Owner* provides essential information about pricing your house, marketing it, writing a contract and going through escrow.
**$24.95/FSBO**

## Homestead Your House

*Attorneys Ralph Warner, Charles Sherman*
*& Toni Ihara*
*California 8th Edition*
This book shows you how to file a Declaration of Homestead and includes complete instructions and tear-out forms.
**$9.95/HOME**

## LANDLORDS & TENANTS

## The Landlord's Law Book, Vol. 1: Rights & Responsibilities

*Attorneys David Brown & Ralph Warner*
*California 3rd Edition*
This book contains information on deposits, leases and rental agreements, inspections (tenants' privacy rights), habitability (rent withholding), ending a tenancy, liability and rent control.
**$29.95/LBRT**

## The Landlord's Law Book, Vol. 2: Evictions

*Attorney David Brown*
*California 3rd Edition*
Updated for 1992, this book will show you step-by-step how to go to court and get an eviction for a tenant who won't pay rent—and won't leave. Contains all the tear-out forms and necessary instructions.
**$29.95/LBEV**

## Tenants' Rights

*Attorneys Myron Moskovitz &*
*Ralph Warner*
*California 11th Edition*
This book explains how to handle your relationship with your landlord and understand your legal rights when you find yourself in disagreement. A special section on rent control cities is included.
**$15.95/CTEN**

## JUST FOR FUN

## 29 Reasons Not to Go to Law School

*Attorneys Ralph Warner & Toni Ihara*
*National 3rd Edition*
Filled with humor and piercing observations, this book can save you three years, $70,000 and your sanity.
**$9.95/29R**

## Devil's Advocates: The Unnatural History of Lawyers

*by Andrew & Jonathan Roth*
*National 1st Edition*
This book is a painless and hilarious education, tracing the legal profession. Careful attention is given to the world's worst lawyers, most preposterous cases and most ludicrous courtroom strategies.
**$12.95/DA**

## Poetic Justice: The Funniest, Meanest Things Ever Said About Lawyers

*Edited by Jonathan & Andrew Roth*
*National 1st Edition*
A great gift for anyone in the legal profession who has managed to maintain a sense of humor.
**$8.95/PJ**

## OLDER AMERICANS

## Elder Care: Choosing & Financing Long-Term Care

*Attorney Joseph Matthews*
*National 1st Edition*
This book will guide you in choosing and paying for long-term care, alerting you to practical concerns and explaining laws that may affect your decisions.
**$16.95/ELD**

## Social Security, Medicare & Pensions

*Attorney Joseph Matthews with*
*Dorothy Matthews Berman*
*National 5th Edition*
This book contains invaluable guidance through the current maze of rights and benefits for those 55 and over, including Medicare, Medicaid and Social Security retirement and disability benefits and age discrimination protections.
**$15.95/SOA**

**N O L O   P R E S S   /   9 5 0   P A R K E R   S T R E E T   /   B E R K E L E Y   C A   9 4 7 1 0**

# O R D E R   F O R M

Name

Address (UPS to street address, Priority Mail to P.O. boxes)

| Catalog Code | Quantity | Item | Unit price | Total |
|---|---|---|---|---|
| | | | | |
| | | | | |
| | | | | |
| | | | | |
| | | | | |
| | | | | |
| | | | | |
| | | Subtotal | | |
| | | Sales tax (California residents only) | | |
| | | Shipping & handling | | |
| | | 2nd day UPS | | |
| | | TOTAL | | |

**SALES TAX**
California residents add your local tax

**SHIPPING & HANDLING**
$4.00     1 item
$5.00     2-3 items
+$.50     each additional item
Allow 2-3 weeks for delivery

**IN A HURRY?**
UPS 2nd day delivery is available:
Add $5.00 (contiguous states) or
$8.00 (Alaska & Hawaii) to your regular shipping and handling charges

**PRICES SUBJECT TO CHANGE**

**FOR FASTER SERVICE, USE YOUR CREDIT CARD AND OUR TOLL-FREE NUMBERS:**
Monday-Friday, 7 a.m. to 5 p.m. Pacific Time
Order line                          1 (800) 992-6656
General Information          1 (510) 549-1976
Fax us your order              1 (800) 645-0895

**METHOD OF PAYMENT**
☐ Check enclosed    ☐ VISA  ☐ Mastercard
☐ Discover Card       ☐ Amer ican Express

Account #                                      Expiration Date

Signature Authorizing

Phone                                                      PAGI1

**N O L O   P R E S S   /   9 5 0   P A R K E R   S T R E E T   /   B E R K E L E Y   C A   9 4 7 1 0**